WHAT THE
ROMANS
DID FOR US

WHAT THE
ROMANS
DID FOR US

PHILIP WILKINSON

FOREWORD BY ADAM HART-DAVIS

BOXTREE

First published in 2000 by Boxtree, an imprint of Macmillan Publishers Ltd,
25 Eccleston Place, London SW1W 9NF and Basingstoke

Associated companies throughout the world

ISBN 0 7522 1902 2

Text copyright © 2000 Philip Wilkinson

The right of Philip Wilkinson to be identified as the author of this work
has been asserted by him in accordance with the Copyright, Designs
and Patents Act 1988.

9 8 7 6 5 4 3 2 1

A CIP catalogue record for this book is available from the British Library

Design by Jane Coney

Colour reproduction by Aylesbury Studios Ltd

Printed by Bath Press Ltd, Bath

By arrangement with the BBC

Presented by Adam Hart-Davis
Series Producer - Martin Mortimore
Series Researcher - Paul King
Executive Producer - Caroline van den Brul

The BBC logo is a trademark of the British Broadcasting Corporation and is
used under licence.
BBC logo © BBC 1996.

PHOTOGRAPH ACKNOWLEDGEMENTS

14, 20, 23, 24, 27 by Ken Green: 6, 62, 77, 78, 79, 122, 123 by Mark Pinder;
12 & 42 map artwork by Brian Borthwick; 52, 60, 43, 124, 125, 144 by Sian
Griffiths; 33, 52, 110, 12 by Paul King; 88, 133 by Martin Mortimore; 72,
108, 109 by Inge Samuels. All courtesy of the BBC.
8, 18, 46 courtesy of AKG London; FRONTISPIECE, 11, 19, 25, 29, 51, 67, 68,
72, 89, 102, 105, 107, 117, 119, 134, 137, 141, 142, 148, 13 courtesy of
the Ancient Art & Architecture Collection; 16, 35, 64, 71, 93 courtesy of the
Art Archive; 145 courtesy of The British Museum; 54 courtesy of CM Dixon;
17, 19, 39, 48, 49, 55, 66, 81, 88, 94-95, 97, 98-99, 113, 115, 116, 120,
126, 131, 143 courtesy of English Heritage; 30, 31, 32, 132 by Pete Jones;
104, 147 courtesy of the Museum of London; 58 courtesy of National
Museum of Wales; 150 courtesy of Staatliches Konservatoramt, Germany.

CONTENTS

▲ ADAM HART-DAVIS
JOURNEYS TO THE EDGE OF
THE ROMAN EMPIRE AT
HADRIAN'S WALL.

FOREWORD

Shooting the series *What The Romans Did For Us* has been a fascinating experience – every day I have learned something new. I had heard about their central heating – the hypocaust – but I had no idea that the Romans introduced apples and pears to this country. I knew that Roman roads are straight, but I did not know how they managed to set off in just the right direction. For example, from London to Chichester, how did they work out exactly which way to go without a map or a compass? I discovered the answer tramping over sand dunes with beacons and a simple surveying instrument, a groma. One of the beacons dripped candlewax on my new fleece, and I got soaked by the rain, but we had a great time.

I learned most of all from the wonderful wooden machines that were specially built by Henry and John Russell – the wine press, the odometer, and especially the waterwheel. When the gold mines at Dolaucothi in Wales became flooded, the Romans built waterwheels to pump the water out of the mines. Guessing from the fragments that have been found, the Russells built a new one, twelve feet high and a foot wide. I walked up the outside of this wheel like a treadmill, and was able to pump water ten feet upwards, although it was exceedingly hard work. After a couple of minutes I was dripping with sweat, and had to take a rest. The problem was that even my massive weight was barely enough to lift the water, and puny British slaves would have been too light; so we reckon the Roman wheels must have been narrower – perhaps eight inches rather than a foot. What's more, when I did get it going, I was pumping a bathful – 150 litres - every minute, which is about twice what the experts reckon the Roman pumps lifted. So we discovered more about the wheel by using it, and the main thing was that it worked brilliantly. We know now that it was at least possible to pump water out of the mines with such a machine, and they may even have had a series of waterwheels, one above the other, to lift the water all the way to the surface.

An intriguing thing about the Romans is that they were brilliant engineers and organizers, but poor innovators. They came to Britain in the middle of the first century, and built roads and forts, baths and drains, many of which survive to this day. And yet most of their ideas were taken from the Greeks, and they seem to have been unable to come up with new ones of their own. They occupied Britain for 400 years, but in all that time they had no industrial revolution; their technology was advanced when they arrived, but scarcely any more advanced by the time they went home again. This failure to move forward may have been one of the underlying reasons for the collapse of the Roman empire.

Both the television series and this book are based on hard historical and archaeological evidence, but there is still plenty of room for speculation. I hope you enjoy reading the book as much as we enjoyed making the series.

ADAM HART-DAVIS

INTRODUCTION

Central heating and seige weapons, bridges and fire engines, frescoes and fast food – what do all these things have in common? They were all introduced to Britain more than 2,000 years ago by the Romans. The Romans were one of the most technologically advanced people of the ancient world. They carved out a huge empire, and wherever they went they picked up new ideas, which they then carried with them to the new lands they conquered. They also built towns and cities, and these became not only centres of trade but also meeting-points and melting-pots of ideas and fashions that then spread, along the Romans' formidable road network, all over Europe and beyond.

◀ BUST OF THE EMPEROR
CLAUDIUS, WHO ORDERED
THE INVASION OF BRITAIN IN
AD 43.

This book, like the television series presented by Adam Hart-Davis that it accompanies, explores Roman technology and its impact on Britain. It covers both the big ideas, such as town planning and military strategy, and the smaller inventions, such as sewer pipes, which probably had a huge effect on people's lives. It describes many of the places, the forts, amphitheatres, villas, and towns where evidence of these innovations can still be found, and it illustrates some of the reconstructions made for the television series. Rebuilding a Roman siege weapon or wine press is a fascinating exercise. It both helps to bring history to life and teaches us a lot about ancient technology – what problems the inventors faced, how the item might have been used, and whether a design described by an ancient writer could actually have been built.

THE BRITONS

The people who lived in Britain before the Romans arrived belonged to a mixture of tribal groups, some from Europe. In this book they are referred to, for convenience, as Britons. The Romans were a great power and they brought a vast amount of technical knowledge with them to Britain, but it would be a mistake to think of the Britons as ignorant barbarians. They too had skill in a range of technologies. They were accomplished workers of bronze and iron who knew how to mine metallic ore, smelt it, and use it to create fine jewellery and weapons. Their round houses were built by woodworkers of great ability. Their huge hill forts were impressive construction projects, with ramparts and ditches that were great feats of earth-moving. They were skilled horsemen and charioteers. They were well organized in local kingdoms, and had their own coinage.

With such abilities, the Britons no doubt appreciated many of the innovations the Romans brought with them. The luxurious life of the Roman villa, with its baths, gardens, and comfortable, well-decorated rooms, would have appealed strongly to the richer Britons. So would the possibility of easier transport as a result of the Roman roads. And the Romans offered a huge new market for British goods: legionaries needed food and supplies as did those who retired and settled in Britain. Roman taxes might have seemed a price worth paying for these business opportunities. They may have resisted conquest at first, but many Britons soon became converted to the Roman way of life.

THE ROMAN EMPIRE

By the time of Julius Caesar, Rome had a huge empire, stretching from Spain to Syria, North Africa to Germany, bringing together people and ideas from three continents. Caesar himself expanded the empire, conquering Gaul (France), and he also set his sights on Britain. The Roman world knew Britain as a place across the sea that traded with Europe, supplying grain and metals such as tin and buying products such as wine. It was thus a potential source of wealth for the Romans. But there was another reason for the Roman leader to launch an expedition to the island. Britons had come to the assistance of the Gauls when they fought against Caesar. From a Roman point of view, it would be best to give these former opponents a taste of the might of the legions.

    Caesar invaded Britain twice, in 55 and 54 BC. The first expedition was a military failure that Caesar was able to dress up

▾ AN ARTIST'S IMPRESSION OF CAESAR'S TROUPS AND THEIR OPPOSITION.

as a tactical withdrawal, and it brought him much support in Rome. The second was a greater military success and allowed Caesar to extort tribute from the Britons, but it was hardly the lasting success that the Romans wanted, so again they withdrew to Gaul, content at least to have gained valuable knowledge of an island to which one day they might return.

THE INVASION OF CLAUDIUS

Britain was still unfinished business for the Romans when in AD 41 a new emperor, Claudius, came to the throne. Claudius had his problems. Physically infirm and accused of imbecility, he was the only adult male of the imperial family left when the emperor Caligula was killed. The army proclaimed Claudius Emperor but the Senate objected, and Claudius had little support in Rome. He needed a major victory to give himself prestige, backing, and revenue.

So in AD 43 a Roman fleet set off from Boulogne to invade Britain on behalf of the new emperor. The invasion of Britain was a campaign Claudius needed to win, and he threw resources at it. Four legions and probably a similar number of auxiliary troops – a total of approximately 40,000 soldiers – made up the invasion force. Among the

▾ MAP OF THE ROMAN EMPIRE ON THE EVE OF THE INVASION.

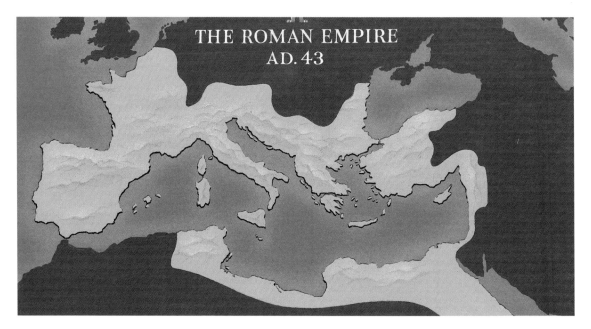

THE ROMAN EMPIRE
AD. 43

expedition's leaders were some of Rome's most prominent men. Aulus Plautius, related to Claudius by marriage, had experience of water-borne operations on the Danube and was a good choice as overall commander. Other leaders included men of the calibre of Vespasian and Galba, both of whom would later become emperors.

For many of those who served under Aulus Plautius, this was a leap into the unknown. The army included men from all over the empire, auxiliaries from places as far afield as Spain and North Africa, numerous Gauls, and some from Rome itself. They were pushing further north than the Romans had gone before, and had to be prepared to face tough country, the cold, and 20 miles of sea.

And then there were the Britons. The native people of Britain had a reputation as ferocious warriors. They would paint themselves with woad and hurl themselves without fear into the conflict. They were used to the terrain and could disappear into the hills, popping out like guerrillas to attack the Romans when they were least expected. The legions knew they had a tough time ahead, going for a decisive victory where the great Caesar had had to settle for less.

On the other hand, the Romans had a huge army that was highly organized. Filing across the Kentish countryside in an apparently endless line, legions, auxiliaries, and baggage trains systematically arrayed, their armour gleaming and their ranks receding far into the distance, the troops must have made an awesome sight. They meant business, and the Britons knew it.

In a matter of weeks, it was clear that Roman discipline and organization would win through. Landing in Kent and marching west towards the Thames, the Romans made light work of the local opposition. They defeated a British force by the Thames, where the Celtic leader Togodumnus was killed. Soon the invaders were heading north to the British capital at Camulodunum (Colchester) in Essex, where Plautius called for Claudius to come from Rome and take part in the battle for this key town. When Claudius arrived with reinforcements and elephants, guaranteed to strike fear into the natives, British resistance caved in, and the emperor was paraded through Camulodunum in triumph. Other rulers from southern Britain soon submitted to Roman rule, and, only a few weeks after landing, the invaders had control of much of the south and east.

CONSOLIDATION

Aulus Plautius stayed on. He became the governor of the new Roman province of Britannia. He consolidated the conquest by building forts and roads, and began the lengthy process of expanding the province. This task went far more slowly than the initial invasion – in fact it took years. During the first three years or so of the occupation, Vespasian subdued the people of Dorset, south Wiltshire, and south-west Somerset. At the same time Aulus Plautius expanded into East Anglia. The next decades saw Roman campaigns in the Midlands and Welsh borders, and these were followed by an assault on North Wales and Anglesey. In about AD 78 the famous leader Agricola became governor of Britain and began his campaign to conquer northern England and southern Scotland. But the whole of Scotland was never brought fully under Roman rule – local resistance, harsh country, and the need to use troops in other parts of the empire saw to that.

Nevertheless, the Romans ruled the greater part of Britain for 400 years. Like any ruling power, they had their setbacks, from the famous revolt of the Iceni tribe under Boudicca in AD 61 to frequent attacks from Angles, Saxons, and Jutes during the fourth century. But the Romans held their ground.

One reason for their success was the fact that they were so organized. As soon as they arrived they built a series of forts as bases for their troops. The forts were connected by a network of roads. Both the army and imperial administrators could travel quickly and easily around. The economy was another factor. Efficient agriculture fuelled the urban population in a series of new towns that were centres of trade. Again, there were ups and downs, but on the whole Roman Britain prospered, and there is evidence that it was doing better than many places when the

▼ ADAM HART-DAVIS MARVELS AT THE WOODWORK OF THE RECONSTRUCTED FORTIFICATIONS AT THE LUNT FORT.

empire suffered political instability and other hardships in the third century.

This organizational side of the Roman empire was one thing that set it apart from anything known in Britain before. Before the Romans arrived, Britain was made up of a series of small kingdoms. These came together from time to time in alliances and traded with each other, but the island was essentially divided, and each kingdom could go its separate way, doing things the way its king and ruling elite wanted. With the Romans this changed. Britain became part of a super-state, and had to fit in with Roman frameworks of organization in many areas – the army with its chains of command, the governor and his staff, the network of towns that became centres of local government. There was a Roman coinage and a Roman tax system, Roman laws and a Roman administration.

A WORLD OF NEW IDEAS

This proved an ideal background for Roman inventions to be taken up, and taken up they were, the length and breadth of the land. The villas were one focus of innovation. Their heating and baths were prime examples of new Roman technology; their decoration drew on an artistic tradition that came from Rome. The towns, with their markets, grid-planned streets, and tall buildings were also centres of the new. Legionary forts, with their pre-planned, and even pre-fabricated, construction and ordered rows of barrack blocks, were another mark of the Romans' new ways of doing things. In the far north of the province of Britannia, the Romans constructed their greatest fortification, Hadrian's Wall. On the south coast, at Dover, they built that most practical symbol of their domination of the seas – two lighthouses. Many of these innovations decayed and disappeared when the Romans left Britain in the fifth century, but much remained. Many modern towns are Roman foundations; our capital city was the chief city of Roman Britain; the Roman road network has survived to this day. On this grand scale and in many small, telling ways they brought to Britannia such new things as apples and pears, toggle fasteners, and bagpipes – the Romans absorbed Britain into their world, and transformed it.

CHAPTER 1

INVASION

The Roman legacy to Britain began on the day in AD 43 when Claudius' invasion force landed in Kent. Never had such a large, well-disciplined and well-organized army been seen in Britain. Never had an outside invader arrived with the purpose of taking over the whole island, imposing new social structures and technologies that would transform Britain from the south coast to the Scottish borders. The Roman legions themselves brought much of this technology with them. From armour and weapons to techniques of carpentry and construction, it took rapid effect and had a lasting impact. The story of what the Romans did for us, therefore, begins with their army – on the march, in its barracks, and on the battlefield.

▲ BRONZE COIN OF THE EMPEROR CLAUDIUS, DATING FROM AD 41– 45.

◀ ONE OF THE CARVED RELIEFS ON TRAJAN'S COLUMN, ROME, SHOWS ROMAN TROOPS PREPARING WOODEN FORTIFICATIONS.

Sailing to the Edge of the World

With their advanced equipment, the Roman legionaries looked powerful, but many of them were scared. To a Roman, the cold seas off Boulogne, where the invasion fleet was based, seemed to stretch towards the edge of the world. The army's rank and file were used to marching to their campaigns. Their experience of sea journeys was mainly in the calm, warm Mediterranean, and many of the soldiers were not ready for this voyage into the unknown. As a result, the invasion force nearly failed to embark at all, and only the encouragement of the emperor's close adviser, Narcissus, brought the troops round.

We do not know exactly what types of ship finally took them on their journey, but the flagships were likely to have been triremes, with their three ranks of oars, ships made famous by the navies of ancient Greece. Most of the troops probably arrived in ships called liburnians, which could have either two ranks of oars with one man to each, or a single rank with each oar pulled by two men. In addition, there would have been broader, flat-bottomed transport vessels.

▼ A NINETEENTH-CENTURY ARTIST'S IMPRESSION OF A ROMAN WARSHIP SHOWS THE CURVING PROW, RAM, AND ROWS OF PORTS FOR THE OARS.

None of these ships represented a great technological break-through, except for the way in which they were steered. Like the Greeks and Egyptians before them, the Romans steered their ships by means of large oars in the stern (the sternpost rudder was still several centuries away). Steering oars like this could be difficult to control, requiring great strength to move them. The Romans therefore developed a pivoting device, similar to a modern oarlock. This allowed the operator both to twist the oar and to tilt it up and down, making steering much simpler. In addition, the Romans fitted the oar with a crank handle, making it still easier to move.

Little is known about how the Romans navigated, but they sailed far and wide in these ships, south to the West African coast, and even along the Red Sea into the Indian Ocean. By the time of Ptolemy, the Greek geographer of the second century AD, maps of the Roman world were being created which, though inevitably inaccurate, were an advance on what had gone before. A journey across the Channel to Britain, fearful as it was to the army, would have held no great difficulties for the Roman navy.

▼ THE LIGHTHOUSE, DOVER: THE FIRST THREE STOREYS ARE ROMAN.

DOVER, KENT

The discovery of more than one thousand Roman roof tiles with the stamp CLBR (*classis Britannia*) suggests that from the second century Dover was the headquarters of the British fleet. There was a fort covering just under a hectare of ground, together with a large settlement, or vicus, outside the walls of the fort. Remains of one house of the vicus can still be seen. Its walls rise to 1.8 metres in places and the painted plaster, with its decorative designs of columns, trees, torches, and figures, has been preserved.

Elsewhere, in the precincts of Dover's medieval castle, are the remains of a Roman lighthouse, one of a pair that originally guided ships into the harbour. This second-century building was originally much higher, its storeys progressively narrowing towards a lantern at

the top. Today, some 13 metres of its Roman walls remain, topped with a further 7 metres of medieval walls. Excavations in the Dour estuary uncovered a wooden jetty and quay dating to the first century, showing that Dover was in use as a port even earlier than the time of the lighthouse. As at Richborough, the fortifications were later rebuilt as part of the Saxon shore defences (see pages 49 and 139).

ORGANIZING FOR EMPIRE

The Britons' first impression of the Roman army would have been of the sheer numbers of troops and the splendour of their arms and armour. Thousands of men marching across the countryside in orderly columns – the infantrymen in their gleaming metal armour, auxiliaries perhaps in chain mail, signallers carrying their exotic-looking horns and trumpets, standard bearers identifying each unit – it would have made a staggering sight, unlike anything that most

▼ MEMBERS OF THE ROMAN RE-ENACTMENT GROUP, THE FOURTEENTH LEGION, ON THE MARCH. THEY WEAR A MIXTURE OF PLATE ARMOUR AND MAIL.

Britons had ever seen. Even on the march, it would have been obvious that the force was well organized. The division into separate units was clear to see. On the battlefield, this organization came into its own, transforming a vast, varied and potentially unwieldy army into a force that could be arrayed with precision and that could respond, in whole or in part, to the ever-changing needs of battle.

At the heart of the army were the legions. These forces were traditionally made up wholly of Roman citizens, although by the time of the British invasion their ranks had been opened up to others. But they were still the elite of the army, and still the troops about which the ancient writers tell us most.

By the time of Claudius, each legion was divided into ten groups called cohorts, each of which was divided in turn into six centuries. A century was made up of eighty men. This made the theoretical strength of a legion 4,800 men. But it was not as simple as this. Ancient writers tell us that the first cohort was larger than the rest, and historians estimate that it probably contained five centuries of double strength, making 800 men in all. This made the legion 5,120 men strong. These were the theoretical figures, but in fact the strength of legions varied, probably decreasing in peacetime and exceeding the theoretical total during major campaigns.

In addition to the legions, there were similar numbers of auxiliary troops. Whereas the legions were the army's trained foot-soldiers, the auxiliaries tended to add specialized skills. They included cavalrymen, archers, slingers, and troops who were experienced in sea-borne operations. Like the legionaries, the auxiliaries were also organized in cohorts (infantry, mounted, or mixed) similar in size to their legionary counterparts.

All this organization had important results on the battlefield. A cohort was a flexible unit, small enough to move around with ease during action, but large enough to pack a punch. The cohorts could take part in set-piece battle-line arrangements, such as the popular arrangement in three lines (four cohorts at the front, three in the reserve line, and a further three at the rear). But a cohort could also move quickly out of one line to join another, or could be shifted to an entirely different part of the battlefield. What seemed like a rigid framework of organization was in fact a very flexible formula.

TRAINING FOR BATTLE

An efficient, highly organized army like Rome's valued training highly. This began far away from the battlefield. Generals knew that their men spent a lot of their time simply marching across Rome's huge empire. The distances involved could be huge, and must have felt even longer to a soldier with a heavy pack, weapons, and armour. An important part of military training therefore consisted of practice route marches. Apart from anything else, these marches were a useful way of keeping in trim. So, around three times a month, infantrymen could expect to go on practice marches of some twenty miles at a time, and they were ordered to complete part of the distance at speed. The cavalry came along too, and were expected to practise manoeuvres on the way. Marches like this helped not only fitness but also discipline and technique. A good general encouraged his men to be on the alert at all times while marching – there was always the possibility that the enemy might appear and attack the marching column.

A vital skill in the Roman army was making a camp by digging defensive trenches, erecting a palisade, and putting up tents for the night. This was another time when the army was vulnerable to attack, so generals made their men practise making camp at speed and under pressure. Fast work with the turf cutter and trenching tool could be just as important as skill on the battlefield. Archaeologists have discovered several sites, such as Llandrindod Common in central Wales, where soldiers practised entrenching camps.

Naturally there was also training for warfare itself. Generals led their troops in mock battles, having them throw clods of earth to give the effect of flying missiles. Techniques like this helped to simulate the danger and confusion of the battlefield, making clear to troops the importance of responding quickly and alertly to orders. This was a special preoccupation of Roman leaders. Legionaries had to listen out for verbal commands and know the meaning of orders given by means of blasts on martial instruments such as trumpets and bugles. These were loud enough, but might not carry well in the noise of battle if the wind direction was unfavourable. In addition, soldiers had to keep their eyes open and watch for signals given by movements of the standards.

A new general would usually be especially keen to put his men through their paces with mock battles, signals training, route marches, and drill, especially before an important campaign. We can be sure that the four legions that came to Britain to conquer the island on behalf of Claudius would have been rigorously drilled before they set off.

ARMOUR PLATING

For hundreds of years, Roman soldiers had worn one of two types of armour to protect themselves in battle – chain mail or scale armour, made of small metal plates joined together to give an effect like the scales of a reptile or fish. Mail gave adequate protection, and it was flexible, allowing the wearer to move with ease, but it could be pierced by the fine point of an arrow or javelin and it was surprisingly heavy – a mail shirt could weigh up to fifteen kilograms. Scale armour was also flexible, but had many weak points where the pieces were joined together.

The alternative to mail or scales was a solid metal or leather breastplate of the type favoured by the ancient Greeks. This protected the upper body, but was inflexible. By the first century AD, the Romans had come up with a workable alternative, the first articulated plate armour. Known to modern archaeologists as *lorica segmentata*, this form of armour was made of a series of overlapping iron plates joined by leather straps.

▼ A DETAIL OF RECONSTRUCTED ARMOUR WITH THE SOLDIER'S MAIL TUNIC AND THE DAGGER IN ITS ORNATE SCABBARD.

To make a suit of *lorica segmentata*, the armourer linked together a number of iron segments to form each basic part of the armour. The shoulder protector was made up of one group of plates, for example, the covering for the chest and upper back consisted of another linked group, and so on. When the soldier armed for battle, all he had to do was to join each of these main sections together by means of straps or metal hooks. The legionary added a helmet, designed to give protection from all directions while still enabling the wearer to see and hear, a pair of greaves to protect the legs, and hobnailed leather sandals for the feet.

This form of armour gave good protection with the additional advantage that it was lighter than mail at around nine kilograms for the upper body plates. It helped make legionaries more agile in battle as well as safer from enemy arrows. It was the high-tech protection of its time.

Archaeologists used to believe that it was only the legionaries who wore this high quality armour. Auxiliaries, it was believed, had to take their chance with mail or scales. But more and more digs at non-legionary sites are unearthing fragments of plate armour. It seems that this new form of armour was too effective to be restricted to legionaries alone. By the time of the invasion of Britain, the Roman skill in mass production was probably put to good use to provide as many troops as possible with plate armour.

For extra protection, the legionary carried a shield. Before the first century AD, this shield was oval, but around the time the Romans invaded Britain, the fashion changed and legionaries began to carry rectangular shields. The new shape must have been more effective when soldiers were ordered to draw their shields close together to form a solid wall during battle.

But more important still was the way in which these shields were made. A wooden shield could be strong, especially when covered with metal or leather. But Roman armourers realized that they could make their shields even stronger by building up the thickness with several thin sheets of wood glued together. The secret of this strength was to glue the layers together so that the grain went in a different direction each time. In other words, the Romans had brought to Britain that most modern of materials, plywood.

WEAPONS TECHNOLOGY

Another thing that made the Roman army formidable was its weaponry – the legions were well armed, and it was obvious. One of the legionary's most important weapons was a javelin called the pilum. Around 2.25 metres long, the pilum consisted of a wooden shaft tipped with a sharp metal shank which itself could account for about half a metre of the javelin's total length. Rank upon rank of

pila, their metal tips glinting in the sun, must have made a forbidding sight to the hardiest of British warriors. And if these weapons looked deadly, they were also very ingeniously put together. The point of the pilum's shank was made of hardened metal and was shaped to a sharp tip. But the rest of the shank was of softer metal, and this was very important. When the soldier launched his javelin into the air, he hoped that its hard, sharp tip would pierce an enemy's armour, or at least stick firmly into an opponent's shield, rendering it useless. As soon as the tip struck home, the soft metal of the shank bent making it ineffectual for the enemy to pick the weapon up on the battlefield and hurl it back at the Romans.

The great general Marius reformed the army in around 100 BC. He noticed that many pila were not bending on impact and were being thrown back, so he ordered the design to be modified. Previously, the metal shank of the pilum was held to the shaft with a pair of iron nails. Marius had one of these replaced

with a wooden peg. On impact, the peg shattered, the shank swung free of the wooden shaft, and the weapon was useless to the enemy.

The pilum was a highly effective weapon. It could pierce both armour and shields, and a shower of pila could check an enemy charge. The Romans followed this up with hand-to-hand fighting with the sword. The legionaries carried swords with short, broad blades and very sharp points forged from layers of iron. Like the dagger that the legionaries also carried, it was a stabbing, thrusting weapon, and generals often encouraged their men to go straight for their enemy's face.

Pilum and sword were the traditional weapons of the legionary. Some of the auxiliaries carried swords and spears, while others were archers, slingers, and cavalrymen armed with spears. When marshalled with the famous Roman discipline, the combination was a formidable force.

Marius' mules

Roman infantrymen must truly have been fighting fit. As well as their arms and armour, they were expected to carry an array of other equipment. The person who took the blame for this burden was Marius. The famous general was notorious for being keen on training, drill, and long route marches. The Roman leader Frontinus, who was governor of Britain under Vespasian, explains in his book *Stratagems* how Marius also wanted to cut down on the baggage train so that his army could move more quickly: 'In order to reduce the size of his baggage train, which was greatly impeding the march of his army, Gaius Marius had his soldiers fasten their kit and rations in bundles and hang them on forked poles to make the burden manageable, and resting easy. This is the origin of the expression, "Marius' mules".'

The equipment a legionary was expected to carry included the following items: a saw, a basket, a pickaxe, a sickle, a chain, a turf-cutter, a dish, a pan, a leather bottle, and personal belongings. The legionary's pack also contained enough rations – in the form of biscuits, cheese, bacon, and soured wine – for three days. Probably not every soldier carried every one of these items, but each would certainly have carried a sizeable burden.

This variety of impedimenta only hints at the range of skills the Roman army brought to Britain. The soldiers themselves supplied the labour for military building projects, from forts to bridges, which were needed during a campaign. Their talents were similar to those of the modern British Royal Engineers. But the legions also brought with them a variety of specialists. Clerks and corn commissaries looked after administration and provisions. Medical officers tended the sick. Site surveyors, master builders, and water engineers organized the building projects. Armourers, fletchers, and catapult makers made and repaired arms and armour. And so the list went on, every one bringing new skills to back up the military efficiency of the legions.

THE LUNT, COVENTRY

This is one of the best places for visitors to get an impression of what an early wooden Roman fort was like. In the 1930s and 1960s excavations at Baginton, near Coventry, revealed the site of a fort that diverged quite considerably from the Roman norm. Most notably, the fort, known as the Lunt, was a cavalry centre. A special circular enclosure, called a gyrus, was built in which to train horses, and this structure gave the fort an unusual irregular plan.

Many of the Roman auxiliary soldiers were cavalrymen from

▾ ADAM HART-DAVIS STANDS BEFORE THE RECONSTRUCTED GYRUS AT THE LUNT FORT, NEAR COVENTRY.

provinces such as Spain and Africa. They were skilled horsemen and they had to be – they had no stirrups, which did not come to Europe from the east until the eighth century. Instead, Roman cavalrymen controlled their mounts with their thighs. The Roman leaders were keen to use these skilled troops to their full advantage, and so stole horses from the Britons for them to ride. But unlike the Romans, the Britons did not use cavalry, so the horses had to be trained. The cavalrymen led them round and round the gyrus, waving spears at them and shouting so that the animals would become used to the noise of the battlefield.

During the 1960s, archaeologists began a reconstruction project during which parts of the fort, including ramparts, walls, a gateway, a granary building, and the gyrus, were re-created on the original site. These timber buildings, which we otherwise only know from evidence such as documents, sculptures, and tantalizing archaeological remains such as post holes, bring to life the structures and atmosphere of an early Roman fort in a way that is unique in Britain.

IN THE FIELD

Perhaps it was the sheer organization of the Roman army that made it so effective on the battlefield. By dividing their forces into small units, and by training and disciplining these units with care, the Romans created a flexible army that could respond rapidly to commands and could adopt set-piece formations with ease. At their most effective, these units could move into and out of positions, creating an impression like a carefully rehearsed ballet, an effect that was a far cry from the aggressive but often chaotic fighting style of the Britons. Onasander, who was probably governor of Britain when he died in around AD 58, wrote a treatise, *On Generalship*. In this work, he advises the general to wait and watch how the enemy deploys his army before making his own disposition of troops. This sounds like good advice, but it implies that the Roman general could expect his men to move quickly into position under pressure, and to obey commands precisely.

Roman generals evolved different ways of deploying their troops which called on this flexibility of response. Julius Caesar liked to arrange his legionaries in three lines of cohorts, a front line, a second line which could act as a reserve, and a rear line which could, if necessary, protect the force from an attack from the rear. Other generals used two lines of cohorts, or used a V-shaped formation to drive their way into enemy lines. Another of the Roman army's well-known formations was called the *testudo,* or tortoise. In this technique, a body of soldiers held their shields together in front of the group and above their heads to create an impenetrable wall as protection from enemy fire.

Lightly armed auxiliary troops such as archers and slingers could be moved around the battlefield more quickly than the legionaries with their heavy shields and pila. They could fire from the front, adding to the assault of the legionaries with their javelins, shoot from behind, or move quickly to the sides to protect the army's flanks. Archers and other auxiliaries were originally seen by the Romans as inferior to the legionaries, who were viewed as the crack troops of the empire, but as time went on, generals saw the value of the auxiliaries as a key part of their well-disciplined, highly manoeuvrable fighting force. It was such an invasion force that gave the Romans their rapid victory in AD 43, and which helped them to keep control of their new province.

▼ SOLDIERS IN THE *TESTUDO*
FORMATION ARE DEPICTED
IN THIS RELIEF FROM
TRAJAN'S COLUMN.

But there was still work for the Roman army to do. To the north and west, a number of British tribes resisted their advance. Many of these people, in Britain as in many other parts of Europe, used hill forts for defence. Sieges therefore became an important part of warfare for the Romans. As on the open battlefield, good discipline counted for much during sieges, but in this type of warfare there was an added technological dimension – the use of a type of machine new to Britain, the siege engine.

Like a modern army with its rows of tanks, the Roman legions could strike fear into their enemies with batteries of martial machines. Catapults, battering rams, ballistae that could shoot deadly bolts – lined up before an enemy fort or city – could force a surrender before they were even used. Such engines could reduce a timber fort to matchwood and turn enemy resolve to defeat.

The Romans were experienced bow-makers and had learned how to make strong, powerful bows by laminating materials together using a technology similar to that of their 'plywood' shields. They also developed the crossbow, and discovered that they could make it larger, and capable of firing bigger and more destructive missiles. From the crossbow it was a short step to the ballista, a siege weapon that could hurl large stones or heavy, deadly bolts. The ballista may have been invented by the father of Alexander the Great, back in the fourth century BC. By the time the Romans invaded Britain, the weapon had been perfected. At first glance, a ballista looked rather like an overgrown crossbow mounted on a stand, but in fact the ballista worked in a slightly

▼ THE BOLT EMERGES FROM
A RECONSTRUCTED BALLISTA.

different way from a crossbow. Instead of a bow, the ballista had a pair of arms joined by the bow-string. The arms were held in two upright bundles of rope or sinew, which acted as large torsion springs and created a huge force. The operator pulled back the string, using a winch mechanism to pull against the great force created by the bundles of rope, until the string was caught by a catch. The operator then loaded the weapon. When a lever was pulled, the catch was released and the string and bolt flew forward at high speed.

Ballistae could be built in different sizes – arm lengths ranged from 60 to 120 centimetres. Modern experiments with ballistae at the lower end of the range have shown that stones weighing around half a kilogram could be hurled some 300 metres. Larger weapons could probably send three-kilogram missiles even further. Modern speed tests have shown that ballista bolts can fly through the air at terrifying speed of around 50 metres per second.

▲ GETTING READY TO FIRE THE REPEATING BALLISTA.

The Romans are also said to have used a repeating ballista that worked like a machine gun with a huge magazine of bolts. The operator turned a handle to work a cam mechanism that drew the string and allowed fresh bolts to be loaded automatically. Continuously firing, it must have been a frightening weapon, but operators did not find it practical. They ended up firing too many bolts at the same target.

Another device that could wreak havoc during a siege was a type of catapult the Romans called the onager. The onager consisted of a strong wooden frame in which was fixed a spring made of sinew or rope, like those that powered the ballista, but this time the spring was horizontal and a single arm was connected to it. At the end of the arm was a sling or a spoon-like container to take the missile. The arm was hauled back, the sling or spoon loaded, and the arm released. The arm flew forward until it hit a crossbar with a crash, allowing the missile to carry on, flying through the air towards the enemy. The name onager, which means 'wild ass', comes from the way asses were said to kick stones back at anyone who chased them. The weapon certainly had a kick, and, like the ballista, could do great damage during a siege. Also like the ballista, it could be built in different sizes; the longer the throwing arm the greater the distance the projectile could travel.

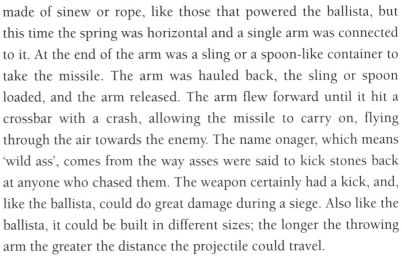

▼ ADAM HART-DAVIS AT THE CONTROLS OF THE REPEATING BALLISTA.

The onager could probably project stones that were larger and heavier than anything shot by the ballista. It would have been especially useful for hurling missiles at enemy fortifications. The writer Josephus in his book *The Jewish Wars* describes the destruction caused by stone-hurling siege engines at the siege of Jotapata: 'the momentum of the stones hurled by the "engine" carried away battlements and knocked off corners of towers... There was a constant thudding of dead bodies as they were thrown one after another from the rampart.' But the onager had a drawback with high fortifications. Because it had a fairly short range, the onager had to be brought dangerously close to high walls, and this could make its operators vulnerable to enemy fire.

Siege engines like the ballista and onager were highly effective, and the Romans used their talent for mass production to build them in large numbers. Vespasian used ballistae on his campaigns in the south-west, and archaeologists have found evidence of the ballista at work during his assault on the great British hill fort of Maiden Castle, Dorset. This fort had massive ramparts and deep ditches, still visible today, but the power of the ballista could overcome these distances and inflict fatal wounds on the defenders. A skull pierced by a ballista bolt has been unearthed at the site.

Weapons like the ballista were not Roman inventions. Roman engineers had borrowed them from earlier military technologists, such as the Greeks, and improved on them. But these machines were new to Britain when the Romans arrived, and probably struck fear into people who had not seen such devices before. Like early cannon in the Middle Ages, the sight of these alien machines was enough to make the Britons shake in their shoes.

There were yet other items in the Roman siege arsenal. One of the most useful devices was the shelter, a wooden construction covered in fireproof material such as uncured hides. Soldiers protected by a shelter could get close to the walls of a fort. From here they could start mining – tunnelling under the walls to bring them down – or could throw up an earth ramp so that they could scale the walls and break into the fort.

If there was no ready-made shelter to hand, the legionaries could improvise. For example, the *testudo* formation, famous on the battlefield, could also be invaluable during a siege. On his first British campaign, for example, Caesar took a hill fort by ordering his men to form a *testudo* and build an earth ramp under its cover. His army was then able to scale the ramparts of the fort. Some Roman writers also mention that the *testudo* was strong enough to support soldiers, so presumably the formation could also itself become the ramp, giving legionaries a quick route up a rampart or over a low wall to pounce on their enemies.

If the main obstacle was a set of walls, the best way in might be provided by a siege tower. Like the shelter, this was a wooden structure, and Roman writers again recommended that it be covered with a fireproof material, such as hides or iron plates. Siege

▲ A SKULL FOUND ON THE SITE OF MAIDEN CASTLE HAS A SQUARE HOLE PIERCED BY A BALLISTA BOLT.

towers could have several levels. From the top, soldiers could pick off their counterparts defending the walls. A wooden bridge could also be thrown out from the upper level, so that attacking soldiers could cross on to the walls. The lower levels of the tower could house siege engines such as ballistae.

The Romans also used battering rams to try to bring down enemy fortifications. Since its use depended on manpower, the ram was normally protected by a mobile shelter. One Roman writer, Apollodorus, notes that once the shelter and ram have reached the required position near the walls, the soldiers should put wooden chocks under the wheels to stop the shelter skidding around as they hurl the heavy ram against its target.

BRIDGE-BUILDING

From walls to ramparts, no obstacle, it seemed, was too great for the legions. Rivers, too, posed little problem. The preferred method of crossing was by fording. If a river was fast-flowing, part of the cavalry would cross slightly upstream of the rest of the force. They would thus break some of the force of the current, making it easier and safer for the others to cross. The troops crossing downstream, meanwhile, could save any equipment – or indeed any men – from the upstream group who might be swept down by the current.

In most cases, fording was enough. But when this method of crossing was impossible, the Romans built a bridge. First the surveyors would look at the site and decide the best type of bridge to build – a pile bridge based on a wooden framework or a pontoon bridge made from boats. Pile bridges could be long-lasting and were suitable in places where the water was not too deep. In deeper water a bridge of boats was the better option, provided that the current was not too strong; this type was also the quicker of the two to build.

For a pile bridge, wooden uprights were driven in pairs into the river bed. Each pair was about 12 metres from its opposite number and the two pairs were joined with crosspieces to form a large trestle. A series of these trestles was built across the width of the river to form the supports for the bridge. The trestles were linked together with further timbers to create a roadway.

To make a pontoon bridge, the army had to carry with it an array of heavy equipment, as the writer Vegetius explains in his book *Military Science*: 'The legion carries with it dugout canoes, or *monoxili*, made from single logs, together with long ropes and sometimes iron chains to bind together these *monoxili*. Once planks are laid over [the canoes], the infantrymen and cavalry can cross in safety rivers that have no bridges and cannot be forded.' The boats were floated to the required positions and anchored in place using wicker crates filled with rocks. Timbers were then laid to span the gaps between the boats, and the engineers laid planks across the timbers to make a firm roadway. Ladders could be placed on either side of the roadway to form guard rails to protect horses and mules as they crossed the bridge.

▾ A RELIEF FROM TRAJAN'S COLUMN SHOWS ROMAN TROOPS MAKING USE OF A PONTOON BRIDGE.

CAERLEON, SOUTH WALES

Part of the Romans' western defences, this town contains many remains of a large, 20-hectare fort. Still visible are lengths of stone wall, which replaced the original wooden defences in around AD 100, foundations of some of the barrack blocks, and a large bath house.

The layout of the barracks can be seen clearly. They are arranged as long buildings which face each other in pairs. Within each block are pairs of small rooms for the legionaries and, at one end, suites of larger rooms for the centurion. Nearby are the remains of circular ovens and a latrine building.

The fortress baths (so-called to distinguish them from another bath building outside the fort's walls) make up a large complex. The walls, plunge baths, and under-floor heating systems (see page 122) can all be seen.

Outside the walls are the remains of an amphitheatre where 'games' and military drill would have taken place. This oval building was the largest amphitheatre in Britain, and would probably have held about 6,000 spectators.

An excellent museum in the town contains a variety of finds from the site, which together evoke a fascinating picture of life in a Roman fort on the western edge of the empire.

▼ EARTH BANKING AND REMAINS OF THE STONE RETAINING WALL CAN STILL BE SEEN AT THE ROMAN AMPHITHEATRE AT CAERLEON, SOUTH WALES.

Roman bridge-building skills were needed less often in Britain than on the continent, where many bridges had to be built to span great rivers such as the Danube and the Rhine. But one area where skills of engineering and carpentry were regularly used was in the building of forts. The invasion force needed forts to accommodate their troops as soon as they arrived. These bases needed to be built quickly and in large numbers to consolidate the conquest. The forts needed both to act as bases, from which troops could march out to quell trouble in their new domain, and to be markers to remind the local people that they had been conquered and that the new rulers were here to stay.

To make the process efficient, the legions used a standard, pre-determined plan for their forts and built with local, easily available materials that could be worked quickly – wood and earth. Later, when the Romans were settled and had the time, they rebuilt many of these early buildings in stone, but to begin with their forts were built at speed in timber.

The first stage was to send out the surveyors to find a suitable site and to mark out the position of the walls with poles and string. The usual plan was a rectangle with rounded corners, shaped like a playing card, but this could be varied to fit the site. When the boundaries were marked out, the soldiers began to dig a ditch and build ramparts around the perimeter. There were several different ways of making the ramparts, which could consist of turfs, earth, or a mixture of earth and stones, no doubt depending on the materials available on site. The total height of the rampart could be as much as 3.5 metres, although some were much lower. On top was a wooden palisade or fence and behind this was a walkway, also of wood, where defending troops could stand. There were also wooden towers and gatehouses.

The Romans may even have prefabricated these structures to make their job still faster and easier. They used neat dovetail and tenon-and-mortise joints again made to standard patterns and sometimes held together with iron nails so huge that the carpenters must have drilled holes for them to stop the wood being split. There was also a standard layout inside the fort, with rows of

barrack blocks to the front and rear, and a headquarters building and commander's house in the middle.

The impression on the Britons when the Romans arrived and started putting up their forts would have been of something markedly different from their own buildings. For a start, the speed and efficiency of the building process, as practised legionaries dug trenches, threw up earth ramparts, and assembled wooden walls, would have come as a shock. Then there was the appearance of the buildings themselves. The usual British house was round and the usual British settlement much more free-form and irregular in plan. Roman forts, by contrast, were rectangular, planned, and standardized. And these outlandish buildings popped up everywhere, for the Romans built forts in a network, at fairly regular intervals (around 15 to 25 kilometres apart) all over their newly conquered territory. The people of Britain had made large and remarkable impressions on the land, as structures such as Stonehenge still show, but the idea that a culture could impose itself over the whole landscape, in waves that stretched from Wessex to Wales, from London to the Scottish borders, and could do so in this planned, predetermined way – this was something new, something indeed that the Romans did for us.

▲ AN ARTIST'S IMPRESSION OF THE FORT AT WALLSEND, ON HADRIAN'S WALL: THE PLAYING-CARD SHAPE AND ORDERLY ROWS OF BARRACKS ARE CLEARLY VISIBLE.

CHAPTER 2

ARTERIES OF
THE EMPIRE

One of the most important things the Romans did in Britain was to build a road network, thousands of miles of well-made roads, arrow-straight for much of their length, all over the country. These new roads swept across the British countryside. Woods and hills proved no obstacle to the Roman engineers – they pushed their way relentlessly along the most direct routes, slicing their way through natural features as they went.

The work of the Roman civil engineers had a lasting impact: the imprint of their roads is still obvious all over the British landscape, in the form of the modern roads that follow the tracks of Roman ones. The line of Watling Street, for example, the road that

◀ CARRIAGES LIKE THIS,
PORTRAYED ON A STONE
RELIEF, TRAVELLED ON THE
ROADS OF ROMAN BRITAIN
AND FRANCE.

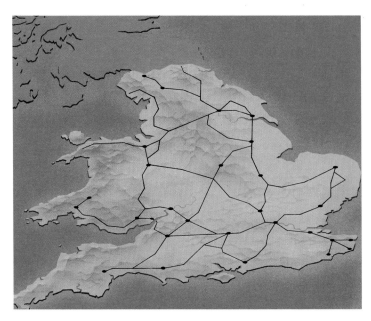

▲ THE NETWORK OF MAJOR
ROMAN ROADS IN BRITAIN.

went from Kent westwards to London and then north-west to the Roman town of Wroxeter, can still be traced as the route of the A5, made up of straight sections for much of its journey from London to Shrewsbury. The route of the Fosse Way, which linked the Roman towns of Exeter, Cirencester, Leicester, and Lincoln, is still followed by straight modern roads for much of its length. Ermine Street, connecting London to York, can also be followed on modern maps.

Of course, Britain had roads before the Romans arrived. British tracks linked villages, fields, and rivers, but these ancient routes were not planned as a whole. What the Romans brought was a road system. The sheer number and length of these roads is astonishing. All over England, stretches of road, often joining towns founded in the Roman period, are still as straight as they were when they were originally built by the invaders. Estimates of the total length of the Roman roads vary widely – many miles remain to be discovered and the figure depends on whether major or minor roads are included. Altogether, however, it has been estimated that the Romans built well over 10,000 miles of roads while they occupied Britain. Some of these were based on the earlier prehistoric tracks, such as the ridgeways that ran along the crests of hills, and other routes connecting hill forts. But more often, especially when it came to the great long-distance routes, the Romans were covering new ground, surveying and building from scratch.

It took organization, clever surveying techniques, and sheer singleness of purpose to build roads as straight as these for long distances, over hills and through vales in a landscape that was largely unknown. Singleness of purpose meant more than anything else. First and foremost, the Romans wanted to conquer the whole island of Britain. The majority of their troops were foot soldiers who marched everywhere. So the main objective in building roads was to provide routes for their soldiers, and the troops had to build these roads themselves. It was tough work, but it may be that soldiers even welcomed it after a dangerous campaign. The historian Livy remarks that at least one general, after a campaign in northern Italy, had his men build a road so that they were not left idle!

Above all, the infantry wanted the shortest route from A to B, and a decent surface on which to march. Gradients did not matter too much, provided that they were not too steep for fit men to march up and down. So the Romans built roads that connected their military forts and bases, allowing their troops to push quickly across country, followed by their supplies. The result was a network of routes which, two thousand years later, still has a profound influence on our road system.

SURVEYING FOR STRAIGHTNESS

How did the Romans manage to make their roads so straight? First of all, it is important to realize that a typical Roman road was not perfectly straight for its entire length. Most Roman roads were made up of straight sections, which tend to be lined up between areas of high ground. More amazingly, the overall alignments of many Roman roads from start to end points are surprisingly accurate, irrespective of the deviations along the way. No one knows for sure how this accuracy was achieved. Roman writers have left behind no book or instruction manual to teach surveyors how to keep to a straight line, although Roman roads are so similar all over the empire that some scholars believe that such instruction books originally existed and have been lost.

On the face of it, surveying Roman roads was not easy,

▼ TO TEST THE METHODS USED BY ROMAN SURVEYORS, ADAM HART-DAVIS SIGHTS ACROSS TWO OPPOSITE PLUMB LINES ON A GROMA.

since they tend to go up hill and down dale – there was no way that a surveyor could see the entire route of such a road with large hills in the way. Roman surveyors seem to have used a system of marker points, perhaps made visible by beacons lined up along the route of a planned road. The surveyors probably used a sighting instrument called a groma to line the marker points up precisely and to position further guide points in between them. The groma was such an important tool for the Roman surveyor that it was almost his badge of office, and images of gromas are sometimes seen on the tombstones of Roman surveyors.

A groma consists of a horizontal cross-shaped wooden frame on a stand. From the end of each arm of the cross hangs a plumb line. By sighting across the vertical plumb lines, it was possible to line up objects very accurately. A road surveyor would begin by lighting beacons at the start and finish points of the road, and at strategic places, usually on hilltops, along the route. He would then stand at one beacon and line the groma up with it by sighting across two of the plumb lines. Having established a straight line between the groma and one beacon, he would then use the groma to sight in the opposite direction to the next beacon. By so doing, he would find out whether this next beacon was in line with the first, and if not, the first one could be moved to the correct position accordingly. With these beacons lined up, the surveyor could then move to the next, aligning it in a similar way, and carrying on like this until he reached the end of the route.

Once the marker points were lined up, the surveyors could take further sightings between them to plot the route exactly, perhaps using canes to mark it on the ground. When surveying a long route, it was obviously most efficient to use several surveyors, each man standing with his groma at one of the beacons.

If they hit an insurmountable obstacle – a crag, say, or a steep hill, or a wide river – the surveyors would change direction to another line, using the groma once more to keep it straight. When they had got past the problem they could then change direction once more to bring the road back to the original line, or they could stay on the new line. There were many places where these detours happened. In Kent, for example, Watling Street made a diversion to cross the River Medway, while the road from Dover to Canterbury had to bend to avoid the steepest slope of Lydden Hill. Modern road maps still reveal these diversions from the straight line planned by Roman engineers two thousand years ago.

All of this seems to have been quite straightforward with the right expertise, and was not highly labour intensive. You needed surveyors with their gromas at several points – often a series of hilltops – and some helpers to manage the beacons or canes for marking. The really hard work came with the construction of the roadway itself.

ROAD-BUILDING

Great builders as they were, the Romans put as much effort into constructing roads as they did into high-profile projects like temples and amphitheatres. The Roman writer Vitruvius, in his *Ten Books on Architecture*, wrote an account of an 'ideal' Roman road which was built in layers. A foundation of large stones (the *statumen*) was followed by a layer of smaller stones (the *rudus*), and a layer of gravel (the *nucleus*); on the very top was a surface of large paving stones (the *pavimentum*). The whole structure could be as much as one metre deep. Because Vitruvius sets this pattern out so systematically, and because he is such a good source for many aspects of Roman building, people have often assumed that his method was the one standard way in which the Romans built their roads. Many books about the Romans contain diagrams of road cross-sections, showing the different layers of this 'typical' Roman road.

Archaeology has revealed, however, that there were many variations. Clearly, different conditions on the ground, together with different locally available materials, meant that the Roman engineers found a variety of ways of building good roads. There were also differences in width, which could vary from four to nine metres according to the importance of the road. Nevertheless, there were several key requirements wherever you were: a solid foundation, a decent surface, and good drainage so that rainwater did not wash the road away.

One common pattern, as indicated above, consists of layers of gravel topped with flat stone paving to provide a surface.

Sometimes the gravel is rammed together, sometimes it is mixed with clay and mortar to make a sort of concrete. Other materials, such as bits of broken tile, could be mixed with the gravel. The paving was cambered, so that rainwater ran off, and ditches were usually provided on either side to take it away. In Britain, however, there was frequently no paving, and a surface was created by ramming gravel down and mixing it with smaller stones and earth to make a smooth top.

Often the road was raised above the surrounding countryside on a bank called an agger. Aggers varied greatly in height. Some were earth banks raised only slightly off the ground. Others were more elaborate structures in which rubble, gravel, and clay were mixed with earth to make a solid base for the road, which stood a metre or more proud of the surrounding ground level. One advantage of the agger was that it gave the marching troops a good view. Roman generals were well aware that their men could be at their most vulnerable to attack during a long march through unfamiliar country. With the agger, at least they could see the enemy coming.

▼ A ROMAN STONE-PAVED LANE IN THE ITALIAN CITY OF POMPEII: BRITISH TOWN STREETS WOULD ALSO HAVE BEEN PAVED.

Ackling Dyke, near Blandford Forum, Dorset, is one place where an outstanding Roman agger is still visible. The modern A354 joins the alignment of the Roman road at Woodyates, a village 12 miles north-east of Blandford, before it veers away towards the modern town. A mile or so further south the Roman agger can be seen, standing out against the line of the hills and going straight as a die as far as the hill fort of Badbury Rings. The agger here is huge, some 12 metres wide and 1.5 to 1.8 metres high: it is a stunning sight. No one knows for sure why the Romans built such a substantial agger along this stretch of road. The area is well drained, so it was not needed to keep off the water. Perhaps it was simply to impress the locals.

There were other variations on the 'typical' cross-section of the Roman road. If they wanted to cross marshy ground, for example, the Romans built a wooden framework on which could be laid hundreds of tree trunks. On top of the tree trunks they built a surface of flat stones, and on top of this they placed a layer of gravel mixed with pebbles to make a serviceable road surface.

When they dig on the site of a Roman road, archaeologists sometimes find many extra layers, one on top of the other. This is because Roman roads needed repairing, just like the roads of today. When a well-used road started to wear out, builders would lay a new surface on top of the old, and this often happened two or three times during the course of the Roman occupation of Britain, creating an underground 'layer cake' of gravel and stones. Occasionally Roman milestones are found with inscriptions that record the date of the repair.

There could have been various reasons for the difference between the European roads, paved with flat stones, and the British roads, with their surfaces of rammed gravel (what engineers call a 'metalled' surface). Cutting and transporting heavy stone blocks would have added to the labour and time needed for construction. In addition, a smooth top layer of rammed gravel would have made a better surface for unshod horses, mules, and wooden-wheeled carts. In Europe, it had been customary to provide a soft verge for this type of traffic, but in towns or in confined spaces there was no room for a verge. Perhaps a metalled surface was a good working compromise.

Many Roman roads in Italy had parallel tracks which probably fitted cartwheels. No doubt similar tracks would have survived in

Britain, had not so many Roman roads been repaired and replaced, one generation after the next. Wheel ruts were obviously very familiar to the satirical poet Juvenal, who uses them in a metaphor when he talks about young men 'dragged along the established ruts of ancient vice'.

WHEELDALE MOOR

This is the site of some of the island's most spectacular ancient road remains. Experts are not certain whether or not they are Roman – they may even be older. A stretch of road some 1.2 kilometres in length is preserved. Today the surface of this road is covered with large stones, giving the appearance of a paved road, but this may not be how it originally looked. These large stones could have been part of the foundations, originally covered with rammed earth and gravel, which have been washed away over the centuries. In some places kerb stones are still visible. Another notable feature is the drainage culverts, with cover stones, towards the eastern end of this length of road.

▼ THE ANCIENT ROAD AT WHEELDALE MOOR, YORKSHIRE.

RICHBOROUGH, KENT

North of Sandwich on the eastern coast of Kent, Richborough had a natural harbour at the time of the Claudian invasion, and was almost certainly the Romans' first landing-place. When they arrived, the Romans dug a pair of parallel ditches to defend their beachhead. Soon afterwards, they established a supply base here, building wooden granaries and other storage buildings. Archaeologists have excavated the area and found where these buildings stood, and plans of several of them are marked out in concrete on the ground.

By AD 85, Richborough was an important port, and was seen by the Romans as the entrance to their province. They built a massive triumphal arch, clad in imported white marble, foundations of which are still visible at the site. From here, anyone arriving in Britain joined Watling Street, the Roman road that led north-east to London and other important Roman towns beyond.

By the third century, Richborough had lost its importance as a port to nearby Dover, but the settlement still had a role to play in the Roman defence system. It became part of the network of defences against possible Saxon invasions (see page 139), and its walls were rebuilt in stone. The massive walls of this Saxon-shore fort still stand, making Richborough one of the most impressive of Roman sites.

The triumphal arch became a signal tower in the third century, but was eventually demolished – it had no role in a Saxon-shore fort. On the ground are the remains of the paved way through the arch, so visitors can appreciate the size of the structure. Some idea of its decoration can be gained from fragments preserved in the site museum – the rest of the stone was robbed and re-used.

▼ THE MASSIVE TRIPLE DITCHES AT RICHBOROUGH WERE BUILT IN THE THIRD CENTURY TO DEFEND THE SITE FROM SAXON RAIDERS.

THE EXPANDING NETWORK

The first Roman roads in Britain were almost certainly built in Kent, taking troops inland from the invaders' first landing-place at Richborough. From here roads stretched to Canterbury and other inland centres, and onwards towards London, beyond which lay the ancient British capital at Camulodunum (Colchester). Richborough remained important to the Romans. During the early period of the occupation, they saw it as the 'gateway' to the province of Britannia, where the road system began. A large triumphal archway was built, and clad in bright white marble specially imported from Europe it would have stood out for miles around, an arresting symbol that stamped the Roman corporate identity on the new province. The archway led to the first Roman street, from which visitors – a new legion arriving for service or a merchant on business – could travel deep into the province.

As the Romans advanced they built their network of forts, and these were linked by more roads. Soon the army could march into every part of Britain with the exception of the far west (Devon, Cornwall, and west Wales) and the far north. Once a detachment of soldiers had arrived at its new base, the roads were ideal arteries that helped them communicate with the Roman authorities elsewhere. One method of doing this was via the Roman postal system or *cursus publicus*, which had been set up by the Emperor Augustus. It worked by means of horse-drawn carriages or dispatch riders who travelled in relays up and down major roads. Every so often there were places, often near forts, where the couriers who worked on this service could rest, change horses, and pick up mail. The *cursus publicus* provided one very real way in which the road network could hold the sprawling Roman empire together. More than this, it provided high-speed communications for the Roman world. A courier could easily cover the thirty miles between one staging-post and another in a day, going faster and further than many Britons would have gone in a lifetime. Good communications like this were vital for Roman government. A state the size of the Roman empire would have been well-nigh impossible without its road network – it certainly would not have lasted as long as it did.

ROMAN LONDON

London grew quickly after the invasion to become Britain's most important city. It was both the headquarters of the provincial governor and the island's largest port. Excavations over the years have revealed the remains of various buildings many feet below today's ground level, but most of these have been covered by later structures. The city was north of the River Thames, in the area now occupied by the City of London. At its heart was a large forum, north of modern Lombard Street and Fenchurch Street, which contained Roman Britain's biggest basilica, a building more than 500 feet long. To the south, near the river, was the governor's palace, which had a garden with a 100-foot-long pool. Nothing can now be seen of either of these buildings, and this also goes for London's no doubt numerous baths (some of which have been excavated) and all but one of the temples. The exception is the Temple of Mithras, which has been reconstructed in Queen Victoria Street. Another interesting survival is the remains of a Roman house preserved in a special inspection chamber in Lower Thames Street.

The only substantial remains above ground are parts of the Roman city walls. These include part of the riverside defences at the Tower of London (the foundations of one of the medieval towers here are also built on the remains of a Roman bastion). Sections of wall that are visible include further stretches north of the Tower and parts of the Cripplegate fort, built on a site north and south of modern Old Street.

The best evidence of Roman London, however, is to be found in the superb collections of the Museum of London. The displays embrace the Roman army, the port of London, Roman sculpture, the Bucklersbury Mosaic (a large geometrically patterned floor mosaic), and numerous displays of other artefacts including items – from tools to jewellery, to a reconstructed city street – that evoke the daily life of the people.

▲ THE REMAINS OF A ROMAN BASTION AT THE BARBICAN, LONDON.

ROADS AND MEASUREMENT

Straight roads had an additional important advantage. They were easy to measure, and their straightness made it simple to calculate the area of the land between them. This could be beneficial when it came to levying taxes, which were often based on the area of land held by the locals.

To help travellers work out distances, the Romans introduced the milestone. They put up stone pillars every Roman mile (which was shorter than the modern mile), so people could see how far they had travelled and how far they still had to go to reach their destination. Sometimes these stones recorded additional information, such as the date and builder of a road, that is now invaluable to archaeologists. Even simple milestones with their distances between cities were an important advance, giving people in Britain a clear idea of journey times and of the size of their island.

A straight road was easy to measure, but what if the road-builder had to introduce a bend to change direction around an obstacle? Pacing out the distance was one solution, but it was never very accurate. The Roman writer Vitruvius suggested a solution – the mechanical odometer. The term odometer comes from two Greek words – *hodos*, 'way', and *metron*, 'measure' – and Vitruvius says that the device had been passed down from an earlier generation, so perhaps it was originally an ancient Greek invention.

As described by Vitruvius, the idea was to make a device that was attached to a carriage and linked up to one of the vehicle's wheels. By measuring the number of rotations of the carriage wheel, it would be possible to turn this

▾ ADAM HART-DAVIS AT THE HELM OF THE RECONSTRUCTED ODOMETER – AN INGENIOUS MACHINE USED FOR MEASURING DISTANCES.

figure into the distance travelled along the ground, as does the odometer, or 'mileometer', fitted in a modern car. The carriage wheels were connected by a series of gears to a mechanism which dropped pebbles into a wooden box. Vitruvius describes how the system of gears was set up so that the odometer 'scaled down' the movement of the carriage wheels. This meant that the carriage had to travel a whole Roman mile before a single pebble was dropped into the box.

At the top of the odometer was a horizontal gear pierced with holes containing the small stones. After the vehicle had travelled one mile, this upper gear moved slightly, aligning one of the stones with a hole below, so that the pebble dropped into the box. The same thing happened at the end of the next mile, and so on. At the end of the journey, one simply emptied the box and counted the stones.

Vitruvius' odometer would have worked in principle, but it has mystified scholars because it involved a gear wheel with 400 teeth. To work in practice, scholars argued, such a gear would have had to be enormous – much bigger than would have been practicable on the back of any normal carriage. The likely solution, proposed by engineer André Sleeswyk, was that the gear had triangular teeth, not the square ones previously proposed. Such a gear would be much easier to make at the required size and archaeology has shown that engineers in classical times were capable of cutting such gears.

USING THE ROADS

Invaluable for military use and rapid message-carrying, the roads were soon being used to fulfil the needs of traders. After all, the Romans were not going to conquer the country and leave it at that. They wanted to take maximum economic advantage of their conquest. So where the legions went, the merchants followed, bringing supplies for the troops and looking for the new trading opportunities that the province of Britannia offered. Soon Britain's extensive network of Roman roads became part of the empire's trade network. Many Roman sites yield evidence of this trade. Take pottery, for example. The Britons had made pots for millennia before the

▲ SAMIAN WARE, WITH ITS BEAUTIFUL RAISED DECORATION, WAS IMPORTED FROM FRANCE AND THE RHINELAND.

Romans arrived, and they continued to make simple clay pots for everyday use. There was usually a local potter who could supply people's day-to-day needs. But if a Roman – or a Romanized Briton – wanted high quality tableware, this was likely to come from further afield.

Britain had two well-known centres of quality pottery. In the New Forest area in Hampshire, potters made a dark-coloured ware, often adorned with paler decoration. Around Castor in Northamptonshire, a style of pottery with raised decoration was produced. Both of these wares were widely admired and traded all over southern Britain. But the best pottery of all came from France and the Rhineland, where potters produced huge quantities of Samian ware, beautiful, red-glazed pottery embossed with elegant raised decoration. Large amounts of this fine pottery were imported during the first two centuries of Roman rule, and it would have been carried along the main roads from town to town as well as along the narrower routes to wealthy families in their country villas.

There were also exports. By the time of the emperor Diocletian (245–313), for example, cloth was being exported in quantity from Britain to the eastern empire. No doubt the road network played a key part in gathering the material together and sending it to Channel ports such as Dover.

By allowing products and produce to be transported with ease, the Roman roads also helped fashions spread around the province. As time went on, more and more people came to admire the classical design of items, including jewellery and vessels, that had first been produced by immigrant workers and had been distributed around Britain along the road network. The roads helped Britons to become more and more Romanized.

ROMAN MINING

The Romans may have had high hopes of Britain's mineral wealth. They would certainly have known about the island's mineral resources because the British locals traded with merchants on the continent, and perhaps they hoped to use the road network to carry the products of metal mining and smelting. One metal that was especially valuable was tin, which was used for soldering and mixed with copper to make bronze. Tin had long been mined in Cornwall and traded via Brittany. The Graeco-Roman writer Diodorus of Sicily, in his *History* compiled around 40 BC, notes that the Cornish had a long history of tin mining and trading: 'The people of Britain who live in the promontory called Belerium [i.e. Cornwall] are very hospitable to strangers and because of their contact with foreign merchants have embraced a civilized lifestyle. These people work the tin, treating the earth that bears it ingeniously.'

By Julius Caesar's time, though, the Roman campaigns in Gaul had brought the tin trade to an end, and Caesar himself seems to have thought that tin was mined in the centre of Britain. In his *Gallic War*, Caesar says, 'In the British midlands white lead [i.e. tin] is found, iron near the coasts, but there is little of it. The Britons use imported bronze.' For a long while, the Romans did not need to be any the wiser, since they had a rich source of the metal in Spain. In the third century, however, Spanish tin was exhausted, and the Romans finally turned to Cornwall's tin mines. They also drew on copper from North Wales, mixing it with tin to produce bronze, for items such as sculptures, jewellery, medical instruments, and wire.

The Romans were much quicker to exploit British lead, which they found in the Mendip Hills of Somerset, in Derbyshire, Shropshire, Yorkshire, and North Wales. Then as now, lead was prized because it is readily available, easily

▾ DECORATED WITH A LION'S HEAD, THIS WHEEL HUB COMES FROM THE VILLA SITE AT LULLINGSTONE, KENT.

worked, and resistant to corrosion. These qualities made the metal useful for water pipes, cisterns, and other parts used in plumbing; it was also used for coffins and burial urns for the same reasons. The Roman army began to take lead very soon after they arrived. The metal was valuable enough (and malleable enough) for ingots to be stamped, sometimes with the date, and the earliest so far discovered comes from AD 49. Soon there was a lead-mining community in the Mendips at Charterhouse that was large enough to have its own amphitheatre.

The Romans knew of an additional benefit of lead mining. They had discovered how to extract silver from some lead deposits using a process called cupellation, which they introduced to Europe. Silver is often found as an impurity in lead sulphide. To extract the silver, the metalworker first heated the ore to get rid of the sulphur. This left an alloy of lead and silver. They melted the alloy in a clay crucible called a cupel and blew a strong blast of air across the molten metal. This process separated the silver from the lead, leaving a shiny deposit of silver. The Romans valued silver for items such as spoons and also for plating some bronze objects.

Iron was mined on an even larger scale and there were mines in the Midlands, North Wales, the Forest of Dean, and the Sussex Weald. Iron was used widely by the Romans for everything from tools to legionary armour, and the metal was already being exported from Britain to the continent before the conquest. After the Romans arrived they took advantage of this rich supply of iron, using it to make equipment for the army based in Britain and, no doubt, sending it across the Channel. In addition, the Romans introduced improved furnaces to make the smelting process more efficient.

Iron smelting required fuel, and the most common fuels were wood and charcoal. There was also coal, although much of it contained too much sulphur to be good for smelting. An exception was the sea coal picked up on the north-west coast which might have been used by smelters working near Hadrian's Wall. But coal was widely used as a fuel for heating, especially for firing hypocausts, the under-floor heating systems used in bath houses. As a result, there were thriving miners, both in Somerset and in northern England, who gathered coal from the surface.

GOLD MINING

More glamorous than these products were the minerals used in jewellery. Jet from Whitby in Yorkshire and shale from Dorset were both polished for jewellery, but most glamorous of all was gold. The Romans may have had high hopes of British gold, since items made of the metal had found their way into the empire from Britain and Ireland. Britain seemed to promise a rich source of wealth. But the truth was very different: there was but little gold in Britain. The Romans seem to have worked only one mine, at Dolaucothi in south-western Wales. They were thought to have opened this mine themselves, but recent archaeological studies have shown that it was worked before the conquerors arrived. The Romans took it over and developed it.

DOLAUCOTHI, WEST WALES

At the gold mine in Dolaucothi, the area of open-cast working and the entrances to the mining tunnels are still visible. The site is difficult to interpret, because it is hard to distinguish the remains of Roman mining from those of later and earlier periods. Nevertheless, it is possible to make out, quite near the entrances to the tunnels, the supporting bank of one of the reservoirs which held water used for washing the ore. Further away, a dip in the hillside marks the site of a larger reservoir. The fragment of the wooden waterwheel found at Dolaucothi is now in the National Museum of Wales at Cardiff.

Mining for gold was a lot more complicated than simply digging a hole and hacking out the precious nuggets. Gold is rare, and the miners were most successful when they found easy methods of exposing seams of the metal and removing the unwanted rock that did not contain any gold. To open up fissures and make the rock easier to work, the Romans lit fires. As the rock split under the heat, it was easier for the miners to reach the precious seams of gold.

This usually left them with a very small amount of metal and a large quantity of unwanted rock. There were two ways of removing unwanted rock. You could simply carry it away, but this was hard, slow work; you might need to move tonnes of rock, in tough, back-breaking conditions, to obtain a few grams of gold. An alternative method is known as hushing. It made use of Roman engineering skill by running water over the rock to loosen and remove the material. To do this at Dolaucothi, the miners built a series of channels, or leats, to bring water to the site. These led to a pair of reservoirs, one of which could hold around one million gallons of water. When the time came to remove a batch of unwanted debris, sluice gates were opened and the water rushed out of the reservoir, taking with it much of the loose unwanted material.

This running water system, designed to carry away large quantities of rock, could also be useful to clean ore which had been extracted. For this process, water cascaded over a number of 'washing tables'. A further use of water was to extract small amounts of gold hidden in the muddy deposits that built up in the mine. For this technique, known as hydraulicking or ground sluicing, a gentler flow of water was required. The water washed the silt through filter beds which trapped the gold dust, letting the silt flow away. The ancient miners tried various materials as filters.

▾ VISITORS EMERGE FROM THE MINES AT DOLAUCOTHI IN THE 1930s.

The stems and leaves of the gorse plant were one favourite. Another was the fleece of a sheep. This technique is believed to be the origin of the ancient Greek story of Jason and the golden fleece.

The mine at Dolaucothi had both open-cast and underground workings, so it involved the Romans in the perennial problem with deep mining – how to get rid of water. In Spain, where the Romans sank deep mine shafts, this must have been a major issue. In 1920, archaeologists discovered evidence of how they solved the problem when they excavated the Spanish Rio Tinto mine. What they found was a 'flight' of eight pairs of large wooden water wheels. Each wheel was operated as a treadwheel turning on a bronze axle and was fitted with buckets which scooped up the water from one level and deposited it about four metres higher up. In this way, the miners could raise water some thirty-two metres from the working gallery of the mine to the surface.

A similar system, on a smaller scale, was probably used at Dolaucothi. In the nineteenth century and again in the 1930s, the mine was reopened and worked. In the 1930s, hitherto unknown tunnels were discovered which contained ancient pit props and a fragment of a wooden wheel like the Rio Tinto wheels. Later these items were carbon-dated and shown to be from the Roman period. It seems likely that the rest of the wheel was burned as part of a fire-setting operation to loosen rock. It is difficult to reconstruct the wheel from one small fragment of timber, but the device was probably similar to the Spanish wheels, and may have had twenty buckets to scoop up water and bring it to the surface.

Intriguingly, there may have been another use for water wheels at Dolaucothi. Some experts have suggested that the miners here used water power to help them break up the rock. The trip-hammer, powered by water, was another innovation that the Romans brought to northern Europe, and a large stone found at the site is believed to be the anvil from such a hammer.

The Romans used a range of other devices for pumping and raising water, although it is not known if these were introduced into Britain. One method, described by several different ancient writers, used a chain of buckets that scooped up water in a similar way to the Dolaucothi wheel. The chain could be driven by a paddle wheel, a treadwheel, or, using gears, by animals walking in circles to turn a vertical axle. Like the water wheel, the chain of buckets was useful for raising water from deep places such as mine shafts.

The Romans also knew about the water screw, a device invented by the Greek scientist Archimedes. The screw consisted of a cylinder with a spiral path running around it, like a large worm gear. The screw was mounted inside a hollow cylinder, and when it was turned, water was forced up the spiral. Archimedes invented the water screw in Egypt, where it was used to raise water in the fields and where it continued to be used on farms during the Roman period. Finally, the Romans had force-pumps, which used a pair of cylinders to raise water up a pipe. These could be used as bilge pumps in ships and to pump water for fire-fighting (see page 110).

(see page 110)

▾ ADAM HART-DAVIS TESTS THE GIANT, RECONSTRUCTED WATER WHEEL DEISGNED TO LIFT WATER FROM MINES.

In spite of these labour-saving devices, mining in the Roman period was an even more dangerous and unpleasant job than it is today. Miners risked their lives bent double in dark, damp, claustrophobic underground passages. Their work of hammering, shovelling, and carrying was exhausting and sometimes yielded little in the way of actual metal. In the early years of the Roman occupation it was yet another task done by the army. Later, the mines were taken over by businessmen who leased the mining rights. Even so, the empire still played a part in the business, and ingots have been found stamped with the name of the emperor. The reforming emperor Hadrian ordered that mines should have bath houses so that miners could at least clean themselves when they emerged into the light at the end of their tiring working day.

UNITING THE COUNTRY

Roman roads had a profound effect on the way life was lived in Britain after the Roman invasion. They allowed the infantry to move around with ease, speeding up the conquest of the country and allowing supplies to be moved around quickly and efficiently. They enabled the authorities to tax the province effectively. They helped trade and industry and contributed to the spread of fashions in the arts and crafts. They allowed messages to pass quickly from one fort or town to another, fostering the spread of intelligence and furthering Roman power. Converging on London, which became the key Romano-British port, they made that city central to the life of the island. They provided, ultimately, a communications link from practically anywhere on the island to the major ports and thence, via further roads on the continent, to Rome itself. Above all, the Roman road system pulled the country together in a way that had not been possible before. To be sure, the disparate tribes of Celtic Britain had been able to travel and communicate, and some of their routes had been in existence for thousands of years. But unlike the Celts, the Romans laid out their roads systematically. The road network, connecting all the major centres, from the forts to ports, unified the province as never before.

CHAPTER 3

EDGE OF EMPIRE

Britain was the northernmost of all Rome's provinces. In the harsh, windswept terrain of northern Britain, the invaders found it hard to gain a foothold. They must have felt like true strangers in the hill country there, where the wind could whip, the temperature could plummet, and low cloud could lose you in a sudden mist. The locals, who naturally knew the country well, could appear without warning, brandishing weapons, or vanish equally quickly into the hills. Not surprisingly, the fourth-century biographer of the emperor Hadrian wrote, 'The Britons could no longer be held under control.'

But the Romans rose to the challenge, building, in Hadrian's

◀ ROMAN SIGNALLING USED SEMAPHORE FLAGS AND EARTHENWARE WATER CLOCKS.

Wall, the most remarkable of all their fortifications. The wall alone makes northern Britain a fascinating place to discover what the Romans left behind. As well as the wall itself, the area yields a variety of other evidence – clues about the Romans' daily life and evidence of how they communicated in this alien environment. The story of the northern frontier is one of the most interesting in the saga of Roman Britain.

THE PUSH NORTHWARDS

During the decades after the invasion, the Roman army expanded the province by moving west and north, building roads as it went and bringing new parts of Britain under Roman control. In the time of the emperor Vespasian (AD 69–79), who had been a commander in

▾ MARBLE BUST OF THE
EMPEROR HADRIAN.

Claudius' invasion force, there were notable advances northwards, and these continued under his successors Titus (79–81) and Domitian (81–96). But it was not easy. The further north the Romans went, the worse was the weather and the rougher the country.

The most famous of the Romans' northern campaigns were those of the governor Agricola (c.77–84), which were written up by the historian Tacitus. Agricola penetrated Scotland almost as far as the Moray Firth, but his conquests were not followed up. The emperor Trajan (98–117), in contrast, concentrated on campaigns in south-eastern Europe. We know little about what was happening in Scotland during Trajan's reign, but it seems likely that men and resources were diverted from Britain at this time. There is evidence that some of the Romans' Scottish fortifications were destroyed in this period, and the Romans may have retreated south to the Stanegate, a road running west from Corbridge, a town which was an important base for Roman campaigns in the north.

When Hadrian became emperor in 117, he saw the need for a more disciplined, better organized approach to the northern frontier of Britain. Hadrian was a reforming emperor. He abandoned Trajan's conquests in the east and concentrated on consolidating Roman power and government in the rest of the empire. He travelled a great deal, seeing at first hand the problems and challenges posed by the huge empire under his rule. He is known to have improved the discipline of the army in Germany, forcing his troops to abandon their alleged life of ease, and to have made sure that his army was better equipped. He is likely to have carried out similar reforms in Britain.

▲ ADAM HART-DAVIS WALKS ALONG HADRIAN'S WALL.

Hadrian saw the importance of establishing frontiers, using natural markers such as rivers and supplementing them with man-made earth ramparts. In the Scottish border country, he conceived Britain's greatest fortification, the wall stretching from Newcastle to Carlisle that still bears his name. The great wall was useful to Hadrian in several ways. During construction, it provided for a few years a focus for the Roman army in northern Britain, a job to be done that could be used to boost morale in the inclement and sometimes threatening conditions of the north. When completed, the wall was a clear marker of Roman power: no one could mistake the fact that the Romans were here and that the territory south of the wall (and even some land to the north) was under their control. It provided a series of bases for troops so that they could respond to local disturbances. It offered an east–west line of communication. Finally, the wall allowed the Romans to police the comings and goings on the frontier. Hadrian's biographer described the purpose of the wall as 'to force apart the Romans and barbarians', but it was not an absolute barrier. There were plenty of gates allowing people to pass from one side to another. When people passed, the Romans knew who they were. The wall helped keep them firmly in control of the frontier.

The structures of the wall

Hadrian's Wall was one of the greatest engineering projects of the Roman empire. It was some 118 kilometres long (a total of 80 Roman miles), and was probably around four metres high. Much of it is about three metres wide. The wall is punctuated, every Roman mile, by small forts, known to modern archaeologists as milecastles. Between each pair of milecastles are two wall turrets, dividing each one-mile stretch of the wall into three equal lengths.

The milecastles are very small. Most of them could only have accommodated a dozen or so soldiers each. Clearly they were not meant to house the whole of the wall's garrison. They are probably best seen as double gateways in the wall, fortified to help in the wall's defence, that could act as bases for the soldiers policing the comings and goings of people who wanted to cross from one side of the frontier to the other. Although we do not know how high they were, it may be that the gates had towers above them that could be used to look out over the surrounding countryside. Such gate towers would also have been useful for signalling.

▾ PART OF THE ROMAN ARCHWAY STILL REMAINS AT MILECASTLE 37, NEAR THE FORT AT HOUSESTEADS. ANOTHER STONE FROM THE ARCH LIES ON THE GROUND.

The wall turrets were smaller still than the milecastles and did not provide a route through the wall. They were more like watch-towers and staging-posts along the wall. The historian and archaeologist Guy de la Bédoyère has noted that it takes about 2 minutes 30 seconds to run from one wall turret to the next. Clearly, soldiers could carry messages at speed by running from one turret to the next and handing over the message to another runner, continuing in relays until they arrived at the message's destination.

▲ At Limestone Corner the ditch could not be completed because the stone was too difficult to remove from the ground.

If the soldiers did not live in the milecastles, where were they quartered? It may be that the original plan was to man the wall with troops based in a number of forts already established to the north of the wall, but when the wall itself was completed, there seems to have been a change of policy. The Romans built a series of forts connected directly to the wall, modifying the wall's structure as they worked. Each of these new forts held between 500 and 1,000 men. These sixteen new forts, together with the others further away from the wall, would have held a formidable garrison.

The wall is impressive for its scale alone, but a wall of this size in this location is still more remarkable. The builders were working in the middle of nowhere; the country was hilly and difficult; the engineers chose a route for the wall across ridges and hills, to take advantage of these natural defensive features. All these things made it difficult to move around during the construction work, and, especially, to transport building stone. Perhaps that is why, in 123 or thereabouts, the builders revised their plans, and finished off the remaining parts of the wall at a lesser width.

Even so, scholars have estimated that the structure originally contained some 3.7 million tonnes of stone. All of this came from quarries near the wall, which yielded limestone for most of the wall's length and red sandstone in the west. Local as it was, this stone still had to be extracted, carried or dragged to the building site, and shaped. It was a mammoth task and must have involved long lines of soldiers, hammering away at the stone, carting and carrying it to the site, and sometimes abandoning it when it proved too difficult to extract.

Not surprisingly, the builders chose a way of working which cut down on the amount of labour needed. They used dressed stone for the outer faces of the wall, building two parallel 'skins' of masonry with a gap between them. When they had laid three courses of stone blocks on each skin they filled the gap between with a mixture of rubble and a cement made of clay, sand, lime, and water. Then the masons carried on with a few more courses of the dressed-stone skins before filling the gap as before. The method cut down on the time needed for dressing stone, laying neat courses of blocks, and transporting dressed stone, and the wall rose more quickly as a result.

No one can be sure exactly what the wall's upper section was like. There may have been a walkway, and the structure may have had crenellations (battlements like those that topped the walls of

▾ AT BENWELL A STONE CAUSEWAY CROSSES THE VALLUM. THIS IS THE ONLY PLACE ON HADRIAN'S WALL WHERE THIS FEATURE CAN STILL BE SEEN.

medieval castles), although these may only have been built at the milecastles and wall towers.

When the masonry was finished, it is thought that the builders covered the surfaces with some sort of white coating, which may have been whitewash or white lime mortar. The reason for this is unclear. It may have been to give some protection from weathering. Alternatively, the purpose may have been to make the wall stand out from the surrounding countryside, as if to give the locals no doubt about the fact that its builders were in charge.

The defences did not stop there. In addition to the wall itself, they added ditches to the north and south to strengthen its fortification. The southern ditch, now known as the vallum, is around thirty-five metres south of the wall. The result was a large earthwork system which created a further barrier, with crossing points near each fort. Anyone who wanted to pass through the wall from north to south, therefore, had to go through one of the gates and walk along the earthwork until they came to one of the crossing points over the vallum. This was an effective way of concentrating all the cross-wall traffic in one place – a sort of militarized zone – and so was another aid to policing.

In 122, when work on the wall began, the site must have been a desolate, lonely place. At the end of the building programme, around 128, the forts were built and the area began to bustle with military activity. In time, this activity would have increased. There would be regular comings and goings between the local communities on either side of the wall. Merchants would take advantage of a large new market and would come to sell their wares. There was lots of bustle, and the voices of soldiers from Germany and further afield must have blended with those of people from Scotland and southern Britain. Today we are used to thinking of the forts along Hadrian's Wall as desolate, windswept places where Roman legionaries would have felt isolated and uncomfortable, but as time went on, the wall would have become a busier, perhaps even a more comfortable place, than it was for its builders and its first garrison. It had a vigorous life of its own, quite unlike anywhere else in Britain.

Inscriptions and Tablets

Life on the wall could be more sophisticated than people often assume. Here, as elsewhere in the Roman empire, there was a literate culture. The Britons who were conquered by the Romans, on the other hand, did not read or write. One of the most important things that the Romans did for Britain, therefore, was to bring with them a literate culture based on their Latin language. This literacy is still obvious at many archaeological sites because the Romans were great makers of inscriptions. Numerous gravestones, as well as stone tablets commemorating the foundation of public buildings, have survived. These inscriptions are often beautifully cut – works of art as well as historical documents.

For everyday writing, the Romans used small, portable writing tablets. The most common type is often called a wax tablet. It consists of a flat piece of wood, with a hollowed-out rectangle in the centre. Wax was spread into the hollowed-out section, and a message could be written on to the wax with a pointed tool called a stylus. When the message was no longer needed, the wax could be heated and smoothed over and the tablet re-used.

Wax tablets were useful for keeping notes and for exercises such as a student's writing practice. Archaeologists have found the remains of wax tablets and occasionally some of the writing is visible where the point of the stylus left a mark on the wood. But because wood decays, and most of the texts have perished with the wax, these tablets rarely tell the historian very much. They must have been very common, however, and archaeologists often find metal styli, which last much longer than the wooden tablets.

Writing styli are often beautifully produced items and were probably often as valued as an expensive pen might be today. They were made by turning a piece of metal on a lathe. The pole lathe had been used for centuries for turning wood, but the Romans took its use further in employing it to shape metal. Using a long, springy wooden pole, and powered by a foot-pedal, this tool made the metal spin rapidly, so that the worker could cut and smooth it to a rounded shape. Once the stylus was perfectly rounded, the worker took it to the forge, where the end was made pointed to make it suitable for writing.

▶ A young woman from Pompeii holds a stylus and writing tablet.

CHESTERHOLM (VINDOLANDA), NORTHUMBERLAND

Although the modern name of this place is Chesterholm, this fort and vicus (see page 99) are best known by their Roman name of Vindolanda. The fort was established before Hadrian's Wall as part of a system of fortifications based around the ancient Stanegate road. It was unused in Hadrian's time but was rebuilt in the time of the northern campaigns of Severus. There was a further rebuilding in the reign of Constantius I, and the traces of buildings that remain on the surface are mainly from this phase of construction.

Vindolanda is typical of many ancient sites in that each rebuilding was carried out on top of the ruins of the previous phase. The floor level therefore gradually rose, leaving the remains of the first fort about six metres below those of the last. The famous Vindolanda writing tablets were preserved in the earliest of these levels of activity.

This site has the best remains of a vicus to be found on or near the wall. These remains include small buildings such as shops and houses, together with two larger structures, a bath house and what may have been a mansio, a kind of hotel where travellers with business along the wall or beyond would have put up for the night. In addition, the well-preserved remains of the military bath house can be seen here. There is also a reconstruction on the site of the original turf wall with its wooden palisade, together with a wooden milecastle gateway.

This reconstruction gives the visitor a clear idea of what the wall was like before the stone fortifications were constructed.

A museum on the site contains a rich display of objects found at Vindolanda, including many of the organic items (made of wood, leather, and textiles) discovered here. The famous writing tablets are kept at the British Museum in London.

▾ A RECONSTRUCTION OF THE EARLY TURF WALL, TOGETHER WITH ITS WOODEN PALISADE FENCE, HAS BEEN BUILT AT VINDOLANDA.

THE VINDOLANDA TABLETS

During the 1970s, a discovery at Vindolanda, a fort and civilian settlement just south of Hadrian's Wall, provided dramatic new evidence of the literacy of the Romans and of life near the wall. Archaeologists began to uncover wooden writing tablets containing personal correspondence.

The tablets found at Vindolanda were exciting even before they were read. This was first of all because they take a rather unusual form. Some wax tablets have been found at Vindolanda, but the majority of the Vindolanda tablets are of a different type. They consist of thin, postcard-sized slivers of wood. Each sliver is between one and three millimetres thick with one smooth surface to write on. No one knows for sure how the Romans made the tablets this thin, but they must have used the same technology that they employed to make furniture veneers. After writing a message in ink, the user often folded the tablet in two, so that the written surface was hidden, protecting the text from damage. In this form, the message could be sealed and sent from one person to another, like an early form of letter and envelope combined.

To write their texts, the people of Vindolanda used ink made from a mixture of carbon, gum arabic, and water, which they applied with a reed pen. Similar pens and ink were used in the southern areas of the empire to write texts on papyrus, the paper-like writing material first used by the ancient Egyptians. In the far north of the empire, where the papyrus reed does not grow, people took to these thin tablets which they made from local alder, birch, or oak wood.

The tablets were remarkably durable after the Romans left Vindolanda. Like many archaeological discoveries, they came from ancient rubbish heaps. Vindolanda and other Roman forts and towns would no doubt have had archives, with stores of tablets held as an official record. But these would have been removed or destroyed when the Romans left. The tablets which have survived were dumped there between AD 80 and 130,

▲ ADAM HART-DAVIS
EXAMINES THE BEAUTY
OF A REPRODUCTION
ROMAN PEN.

and so record events immediately before and during the building of the wall. The further happy accident of damp underground conditions meant that they did not rot away but were preserved, along with hundreds of leather sandals, wooden bowls, hair combs, and wooden tools – all common enough items in Roman times, but which have only rarely survived to the present century.

Most fascinating of all are the texts written on the tablets. Of the hundreds of tablets found at Vindolanda, many are too poorly preserved to allow archaeologists to read anything other than a few fragments of their texts. But a number can be read, if not in full, then enough to give a clear idea of their contents. Reading them was like receiving postcards from ancient Rome.

The texts are written by a variety of different people – officers, soldiers, traders, and slaves – and give insights into various aspects of life at Vindolanda. The tablets contain reports, business letters, lists, and even an invitation to a birthday party. Often they detail items that have been sent from one person to another. Some, for example, concern food. One man writes asking for a selection of different foods: beans, chickens, olives, fish sauce, 'a hundred apples, if you can find nice ones', and 'a hundred or two hundred eggs, if they are for sale at a fair price'. Another tablet lists wooden items sent from one person to another: hubs, axles, spokes, planks, seats, and benches. Elsewhere there is a list of clothes that have been sent: two pairs of sandals, two pairs of underpants, and so on.

Often, as in any modern collection of letters, there is a revealing sidelight about the life of the times. One letter complains about the state of the local roads, and advises the recipient to use mules to bring a consignment of hides. One begs for financial help, another seems to be a petition from a man who claims to have been unjustly beaten by a centurion, a third worries about arrangements for transporting some stone. Another text deplores the disordered, guerrilla-type style of warfare employed by the local British. More than one writer complains that the sender has not heard from the recipient. Remarkably, there are even a few tablets written in a kind of shorthand, another strikingly modern concept introduced by the Romans.

The Vindolanda tablets, of course, are written in Latin, the language that the invaders brought with them. Latin was widely spoken and read in Roman Britain. You had to learn Latin if you wanted to be understood in the empire, and the language no doubt spread as high-ranking Britons became Romanized by educating their sons in the ways and language of the conqueror. The army spread the 'new' language even more effectively. How widely is shown by finds of graffiti at some Roman sites. A famous example from London complains that, 'Austalis has gone off on his own every day for thirteen days'. To understand spoken commands and written messages, a soldier had to understand Latin, and twenty years' service gave him ample time to do so. The Vindolanda tablets confirm that a written culture was firmly established in Roman Britain.

There is even evidence of literary Latin in Roman Britain. One of the Vindolanda tablets quotes a line from Virgil's epic poem, the *Aeneid*, and several of the others may contain literary texts. This concept of a written culture was another Roman import, revolutionary to a people whose stories had been handed down by word of mouth and whose poetry was recited rather than recorded.

▼ THIS VIEW OF THE FORT AT CHESTERS FROM THE NORTH SHOWS REMAINS OF THE BATH HOUSE.

RAPID COMMUNICATIONS

Wooden tablets were an excellent way to send short messages, but what happened when a Roman military commander wanted to relay an order at speed over a long distance? What if there was not time for runners or dispatch riders to travel the length of Hadrian's Wall? One method was to use flags, but these could not be seen over long distances. A better alternative was provided by fire. Fire signalling was an ancient means of communication in times of war. In the play *Agamemnon* by the ancient Greek writer Aeschylus, Queen Clytemnestra describes how fire signals were used to bring news of the Greek conquest of Troy from one side of the Aegean Sea to another. A chain of beacons on mountain peaks and crags allowed the signal to be sent across the great distance.

The historian Polybius (c.205–c.123 BC) discussed how the Romans used fire signals. Polybius, who had been present during the Roman wars in North Africa, knew the practicalities of battle. He realized that on the battlefield, information is vital, both for

▶ SEMAPHORES COULD BE MOUNTED ON WOODEN STANDS ALLOWING ONE MAN TO OPERATE SEVERAL FLAGS AT ONCE.

▲ WHEN SIGNALLING WITH
POLYBIUS' SYSTEM, A
SOLDIER USED A TABLET
TO TELL HIM HOW THE
LETTERS OF THE ALPHABET
WERE CODED.

survival and for morale. 'How can anyone,' he said, 'be of good cheer… or in fact think at all, if he does not understand how many ships and how much corn have arrived from the allies?' But Polybius saw the limitations of fire signalling. Traditional fire signals are all very well, says Polybius, but the two sides have to use a predetermined code if they are to understand each other's signals. Because the circumstances of battle are unpredictable, however, it can be hard to agree a workable code.

Polybius favoured a system that enabled you to send alphabetical signals using five torches. He did this by splitting the Latin alphabet into five sections. Each letter was sent with two signals, one to show which group the letter belonged to, the second to show the individual letter within the group. For example, the first group of letters would be A, B, C, D, and E. So to send the letter C, the signaller would first hold up one torch to indicate the first group of letters; this would be accompanied by three torches to indicate the third letter in that group. The letter F, the first letter of the second group, would be sent by holding up two torches with a single torch. And so on.

Signallers could send messages quickly using the alphabetical system, and Polybius gives them the tip of shortening their messages so that they use as few letters as possible, for the sake of speed. This must have given Roman signals something like the effect of modern newspaper headlines. They would say 'A hundred desert us', rather than 'About one hundred troops have gone over to the enemy'.

The five-torch method could work very well over short distances. Too far away, and it was hard to make out the separate flames – you could see that a signal was being sent but it became difficult to read. So in some circumstances the Romans used a method which relied on a pre-determined code. The content of the message depended on the amount of time the beacon stayed alight. Each party had a list of signals, so if they had a means of timing the beacon, they could get the message.

The Romans used two different devices for timekeeping, the sundial and the water clock. The sundial could measure the hours of the day, weather permitting; it was no good for measuring the short durations needed for efficient signalling. For this, the Romans used the water clock. This was a device that measured time by means of the steady trickle of water through a hole. A mechanism could be added so that the time could be measured on a scale. By any standards, the water clock was inaccurate. Seneca complained that you were more likely to find two philosophers agreeing with each other than two water clocks showing the same time. But it was just possible to use the water clock for timing signals. To do this the sender had first of all to raise a torch to tell the person at the other end that he wanted to send a signal. The recipient would acknowledge and then watch for the sender to raise the torch a second time, which would be the signal for both men to start their water clocks. At the right moment, the sender lowered his torch and the recipient made a note of the time. He then looked at his list of messages, and picked the

▼ RAISING THE BEACON WHEN THE RIGHT TIME SHOWS ON THE WATER CLOCK.

one that corresponded to the length of time the torch was kept raised.

The native Britons may well have used fire for signalling before the Romans came, but their signals probably were not so sophisticated as those used by the Romans. Both of the Roman systems depended on technology the invaders brought with them – in the first case, on the alphabet and spelling system on which their literate culture was based, in the second on the water clock.

The business of supplies

The sixteen forts along the line of Hadrian's Wall each held between 500 and 1,000 men. There were further forts within striking distance of the wall. While it was in active use, then, the wall was manned by a large force. This force needed feeding and, in an alien environment on the edge of the empire's northernmost province, supplying the army was a huge challenge.

This had always been a major issue for the Roman army, which for centuries had been marching into enemy territory. The horses of the cavalry and the mules of the baggage train only added to the problem. Where possible, generals looked for local sources of food for their men and fodder for their animals. This involved requisitioning the supplies and building a secure store so that the enemy could not get them back.

But foraging and plundering was not an ideal way of supplying an army. For one thing, men were vulnerable to attack when they were foraging in an enemy's fields. The locals knew the ground, could predict where the Romans were going to forage, and could lie in ambush. For another thing, the need for supplies could take the army out of its way, spoiling carefully laid strategic plans. If possible, generals preferred a more organized approach to provisioning.

The situation in Scotland was worse than in many areas. With a thinly scattered population in a hard, hilly landscape, there was probably little opportunity for foraging anyway. When the army was on active campaign north of the border, the question of supplies became even more pressing. A large fighting force moving around in alien territory needs still more supplies than a fixed garrison. This was the situation during the third century, when the emperor Septimus Severus launched a campaign in Scotland.

The solution to the problem was to turn one of the forts into a dedicated supply base. The one the Romans chose was Arbeia (modern South Shields), which was kitted out with twenty-two granaries. Close to the sea, Arbeia was in an ideal position for ships sailing up the coast. From here, grain could be distributed west along the wall and north to Severus' troops on campaign.

Further north, by the mouth of the River Tay, was another fort, at Carpow. Some scholars believe this was another supply depot, again easily reached by sea. It could have formed a useful supply centre for Severus and may even have acted as his campaign headquarters. Corbridge, a fort just to the south of the wall, was also provided with many storage buildings and could have been a third major depot. There were granaries here too, together with buildings where equipment and arms could be manufactured.

In the area of supplies as in much else, then, the Roman army brought to Britain a highly organized approach, with storehouses at strategic points. They also showed that they could adapt to local circumstances. The Roman army was used to marching everywhere, bringing its stores along in a baggage train, but in difficult terrain like northern Britain they saw the sense of using water transport, and all these northern bases are accessible by water.

▼ A CORNER OF THE HOUSESTEADS FORT WITH THE REMAINS OF THE BARRACKS IN VIEW.

HOUSESTEADS, NORTHUMBERLAND

Housesteads, known to the Romans as Vercovicium, is one of the most interesting places at which to examine Hadrian's Wall and the buildings that are linked to it. Most impressive is a fort abutting the wall, one of the long sides of its typical playing-card-shaped plan forming part of the wall itself. This fort was home to about 800 infantrymen, who were reinforced with cavalry during the third century. Parts of the walls of many of the fort's buildings can still be seen, including the headquarters building, the commanding officer's house, and a structure which may have been a hospital. There are also remains of granaries, latrines, and barrack blocks. One of the most interesting buildings is the latrine block, where remains of the water tanks and drainage channels can still be seen.

The fort hugs a gentle slope upwards towards the wall. On the levels below, which face south, are the remains of terraces where inhabitants of the fort and the adjoining settlement or vicus grew food. Lumps and bumps in the ground south of the fort also indicate the sites of buildings of the vicus.

Nearby at Knag Burn is the site of one of the gates through the wall. This is one of the few places on the wall where there was a gate that did not go through a fort or a milecastle. There was a double set of gates so that people passing through could be detained within while guards may have questioned them about their business or exacted a payment of duty. Another notable building at Housesteads is a well-preserved milecastle some half a kilometre west of the fort. It has a gateway built of large, well-finished stone blocks which contrast with the rougher masonry of the surrounding walls. Many stones of the archway are still intact.

MANUFACTURING

As well as food, of course, the army needed weapons. They brought many items with them in their packs, although some of their equipment was disposable, such as the iron heads of javelins that bent on impact. So the Romans had to set up manufacturing centres for these objects, and the blacksmith became a key figure in the back-up to their army.

The Celtic peoples who lived in Britain when the Romans

arrived were already skilled metalworkers. They had been working bronze for some two thousand years and for several centuries they had also been using iron. The Romans too were master iron-workers. Like the British, they had to work within the severe limitations of early technology – their furnaces could not reach really high temperatures, for example.

Nevertheless, the Romans had built up a working knowledge of iron and its properties that stood them in good stead. The Roman writer Pliny, in his multi-volume work *Natural History,* notes that there are many different varieties of iron in different parts of the empire. Some are suitable for making items like tools and weapons, where strength is important; some are more prone to rust; others are best used in short lengths for items such as hobnails; still others are brittle and useless where strength is required.

This knowledge was highly practical. The Romans also knew where the best ore was to be found, and used this knowledge to develop an iron industry. There was excellent iron on the island of Elba, for example, and this fed a flourishing iron industry on the Italian mainland at Poplonium. As the empire expanded, the Romans took this knowledge with them, so it is likely that they did bring some improvements in iron working technology with them when they came to Britain.

The iron working process began with the basic raw material – iron ore. First this had to be smelted, by heating the rock in a furnace with charcoal so that the metal melted and could be col-lected. This produced a lump of iron called a bloom. The bloom was brittle and so needed further working to render it strong enough to make tools and weapons. So next the bloom was reheated in the furnace. Then, when the metal was white-hot, it was quenched in water, which hardened the metal further. Roman metalworkers gradually reheated the metal at this stage, to bring about still further hardening.

Then the metal was taken to the forge, where the blacksmith hammered it into shape. This process of hammering improved the toughness yet again. Most forging was done over a fire of charcoal, but in the country around Hadrian's Wall, the Romans may well have used locally available sea coal, a good fuel because it contains less sulphur than many types of coal and so does not introduce unwanted impurities into the metal.

Hammering away like this, a Roman blacksmith could produce javelin heads and similar objects at speed. It was hardly mass production in the modern, mechanized sense of the phrase, but it was production on a scale that Britons had rarely if ever seen before.

SOUTH SHIELDS, TYNE AND WEAR

At South Shields are the remains of the Roman fort of Arbeia. Its position near the River Tyne indicates its main purpose, as a supply depot for grain and other commodities coming from the south by sea. The fort certainly played a military role under Hadrian, but it became a major depot under Severus, when it had only four barrack blocks but twenty-two granaries. Evidence of Severus has been found in the form of lead seals bearing his image – these were probably attached to sacks of grain. There were also seals with the images of Severus' sons, Caracalla and Geta, who ruled jointly.

To give an idea of how both wall and fort might have looked, one of the gatehouses, together with a short stretch of wall, have been reconstructed at full size at the site. With its two large, round-arched gateways, massive twin towers, and small windows, the structure gives a vivid picture of what the architecture of the wall might originally have been like. The reconstruction is based on remains and foundations found on the site, together with a study of evidence taken from other Roman buildings and the carved reliefs on Trajan's Column in Rome. There is no on-site evidence for some details, such as the overall height of the structure, the tops of the towers, and the use of crenellations, but the reconstruction gives as good an idea as any of how the fortifications probably looked soon after their construction.

LIFE ON THE WALL

So the Romans brought a number of new technologies and concepts to their northernmost frontier. This sophistication, together with the information we can glean from the Vindolanda writing tablets, makes Hadrian's Wall in the Roman period seem less isolated and desolate than a glance at the ruins, snaking their way over windswept hills, suggests. After all, the Romans were well established in Scotland before Hadrian's time, and they clearly did not relinquish all of their forts north of the border once the wall was built. They had had the chance to familiarize themselves with the terrain.

Good communications, well-organized supplies, effective building technology and metalworking skills – things like these made life on the wall if not luxurious then at least bearable. Soldiers had decently built accommodation with such prized Roman facilities as bath houses (see page 121). Civilian settlements grew up near some of the forts, and some members of the garrison, coming to the end of their military service, undoubtedly stayed on in northern Britain. And the soldiers and their hangers-on obviously did what they could to protect themselves from the unpleasant local climate. On one of the Vindolanda tablets, the writer reassures his correspondent, 'I will provide some goods by means of which we may endure the storms'.

Above all, the Romans had shown that they could undertake a massive building campaign in a far-away spot, man it, and use it effectively as a way of controlling a border at the edge of the empire. The amount of organization, skill, and sheer manpower needed to accomplish this was awesome, and typical of Roman building projects at their biggest and best.

Oddly, after this massive effort, the wall was not manned for long. By the time of the emperor Antoninus Pius (138–161), a new, yet more northerly frontier, the Antonine Wall, had been established between the Forth and the Clyde. For a while this new barrier, made merely of earth and turf unlike its more famous stone predecessor, was the empire's northern frontier. Hadrian's Wall seems to have been abandoned a mere forty years after construction was begun. But in the 160s the Antonine Wall was abandoned in turn and Hadrian's Wall was reoccupied. During the reign of Septimus Severus (193–211) it was used once more as a base for campaigns in the north. After the Romans left Britain, the wall still stood, an object lesson in the durability of stone buildings – and itself a frequently used source of stone for British builders on either side of the border.

CHAPTER 4

BUILDING
BRITAIN

When the Romans arrived in Britain, they found a country that was already agriculturally rich. The local people lived for the most part in small settlements where they grew crops and raised animals. Using the tools at their disposal, they could probably produce ample food for the local population, with some to spare. Even before the Roman conquest, corn was among the commodities that Britain was exporting to the Roman empire.

But the arrival of the Romans placed an extra demand on British agriculture. Suddenly, thousands of extra mouths needed feeding and the new rulers of the island were levying a tax, payable in grain, on local chiefs. The first response would have been to

▲ WITH THIS RECONSTRUCTED
ROMAN REAPING MACHINE,
THE EARS OF THE WHEAT ARE
CUT OFF BY ITS FRONT TEETH
AND GATHERED INTO THE
WHEELED CART.

bring more land into cultivation, but even so there must have been immense pressure on the technology of British agriculture, which was based on quite simple tools and techniques and could never before have needed to cope with such an influx of people.

PLOUGHS OLD AND NEW

To prepare the soil, for example, the Britons used the plough, which was pulled along by a pair of oxen or cows. In many places, the plough they used was probably very basic, of the type called the ard. The ard is a very simple wooden tool, with a pointed end which cuts a groove through the soil, a shaft that connects to the animal harness, and a handle for the ploughman to hold. It can be made completely of wood, using simple joints. By the time of the Roman conquest, metalworkers had probably learned how to reinforce the pointed end with iron, so that it did not wear out so quickly as a wooden point.

Nowadays we think of the ard as a Mediterranean tool, well suited to light southern soils, though experiments at the reconstructed Iron Age farm at Butser, Hampshire, have shown that it can work well in the heavy soils of Britain. But at some point around the time of the Roman conquest, the plough was improved. One problem with the ard was that it produced only a groove in the soil. For many purposes it is better to produce the 'corduroy' effect we see in ploughed fields today, with deep furrows alternating with ridges of soil. Seed can then be sown in the furrow and after this the land can be harrowed, pulling the soil from the ridge back over the furrow to cover the seed. To create true furrows, a different type of plough is required. A detachable wooden wing, or 'ridging board', needs to be fitted on the side of the plough, to throw up the soil to the side. Ploughs with ridging boards were certainly being used at the time of the Roman conquest and the Romans may have brought them to Britain. We do not know for sure.

Another innovation was a metal blade called a coulter, which was added to the front of the plough. This cut the soil before the ploughshare broke it up. Still another variation was a plough invented in Gaul and described by the Roman writer Pliny: 'A recent invention in Raetian Gaul is the kind they call the *plaumoratum*, a share… to which are added a pair of small wheels; the spike in this case has the shape of a spade. The width of the share turns back the sod, seed is scattered immediately, and toothed harrows are dragged over the top.' New types of ploughs like these must have improved British agriculture, enabling more land to be brought under cultivation.

After ploughing, seed was sown by hand, using the time-honoured method of broadcasting. This gave

▾ STATUETTE OF A PLOUGH-
MAN WITH A TEAM
OF OXEN.

the farmer little control over where the seed fell, or how evenly it was distributed, but an experienced sower could throw seed so that it spread quite evenly and the technique was used throughout the ancient world and through the Middle Ages.

SAVING LABOUR

There was one group of machines that actually allowed farmers to cut down on the amount of work needed to produce their crops. This was especially important after the Roman invasion. The most labour-intensive time on the farm was the harvest, when acres of corn ripened at once and needed to be got in at speed. The traditional way to do this was by hand, using a sickle with an iron blade. In addition, the Romans introduced long-handled scythes, which came from Gaul. They had shorter blades than today's scythes, and the evidence suggests that they were most commonly used during hay-making.

None of these tools would have come as much of a surprise to the Britons. A much more revolutionary innovation was a harvesting machine, which is described briefly by Pliny and at greater length by another Roman writer, Palladius. Although the descriptions provided by the two writers are slightly different, both describe a wheeled cart with a row of metal teeth along the front edge. The ears of corn were caught by the teeth, cut off, and gathered into the cart, which was pushed along from behind by a mule or ox. As Palladius says, the beast should be 'a docile ox, by all means, the sort not to go faster than the pace set by the driver'. Palladius also mentions that the blades of the reaping machine should be upturned at the tips. Blades like this would tend to scoop up the ears of corn, so that less grain would be lost and the blades would be less likely to get clogged. A carved relief of a reaping machine found at Buzenol in Belgium shows upturned blades. The Buzenol reaper has another interesting design refinement. The frame splays outwards to protect the wheels from the remaining stalks, which would otherwise wrap around the axle and stop the wheels turning.

There is no archaeological evidence for the use of reaping

machines like this in Britain, though this may be because the evidence has not survived. After all, these machines were made of wood, and it may be that they were taken apart for other uses out of the harvesting season – the wheels alone could be used in many other ways. On the other hand, the lack of evidence may simply be because the machine did not catch on. It did have several drawbacks. The straw that was left behind was trampled by the ox, so the machine was not much use if the farmer needed the straw; the blades probably got clogged up, in spite of their curved shape; and the reaper would have worked best on level ground. Even so, it could have provided a useful shortcut in times when labour was scarce, achieving in a matter of hours a harvest that would otherwise have taken days.

Looking after the soil

The Romans knew well the dangers of over-cultivation. In the Mediterranean there is a limit to the amount of good land available for raising crops. The Romans were great builders of cities, creating large urban populations that depended on nearby arable land for their food supply. This sort of demand on the land could exhaust it in a few seasons, so early on the Romans learned to look after their soil.

One way to do this was to 'rest' the land by letting it lie fallow in alternate years. Animals could be left to graze on the fallow land, and their manure would enrich the soil, replacing some of the lost nitrogen content ready for next year's sowing. Another method was to use crop rotation. The farmer would plant corn one year, followed by a legume, such as lupin, beans, or vetch, the following year. The legume would replace the nitrogen used up by the corn, and would also provide a further useful crop, either for human food or animal fodder.

The Romans also used a variety of different fertilisers on their fields. Pliny lists many different manures, saying that their history stretches back at least as far as the early Greek writer Homer, who mentions their use in the *Odyssey*. Pliny's list ranges from the droppings of doves and chickens, through the manure of pigs, goats, sheep, and cattle, to human waste products. But best of all, says

Pliny, is 'a crop of lupin dug in with a plough or mattocks before it forms pods, or handsful of cut lupin used as a mulch around the roots of trees or vines'. The writer also recommends certain times for spreading fertiliser – when there is a west wind, when the moon is waning, and when it is not looking like rain; applying manure in these conditions, says Pliny, is liable to make it much more effective.

It is not known exactly how much of this knowledge the Romans brought to Britain. It is likely that native farmers were already using fallow periods and they may even have been rotating their crops; we cannot be sure. But these techniques would have been all the more important in the Roman period as the demand for food from both garrisons and city populations increased.

MANAGING THE LAND

The Roman period certainly saw agricultural changes. There is archaeological evidence for better land drainage, improved scythes and sickles, more sophisticated ploughs, and more variety of crops during the Roman occupation of Britain. But still more drastic were changes in the ways in which the land was managed. This change came about because the Roman empire was a place of widespread transport and trade, and a world in which land-holdings were often much larger than before. The owner or tenant of a large estate could make large profits and was no doubt eager to make the most lucrative use of his holdings. Rich Romans knew this and buying land was a favourite form of investment.

A Roman farmer could increase his productivity in many different ways, responding both to local conditions and the market. It might mean turning more land over to livestock, which was potentially less labour-intensive than arable farming. It could be a case of letting some parts of the estate out to tenant farmers and pocketing the rents. Or it could involve mixed farming of products that were marketable. But whatever the type of agriculture, the farmer had to keep accounts and other records, pay taxes, and plan on a large scale. Once more it was the global, organizational change that was perhaps the greatest of the Roman empire's many legacies to Britain.

▶ WINE WAS TRANSPORTED IN TALL POTTERY STORAGE JARS CALLED AMPHORAE.

INDUSTRIAL BUILDINGS

One piece of evidence for the scale of Roman arable farming is the large granaries constructed by the invaders. As we have seen, forts had granaries. There were also granaries at many villas, where grain from the big estates was stored. These were substantial, rectangular buildings, frequently raised on short stone pillars or wooden posts to improve ventilation by allowing air to circulate beneath. In Britain, granaries were often built with opening vents on the north and east sides of the structure; south and west vents were avoided because of the damp winds that blew from these points of the compass.

Another innovation in farm building was the kiln used to dry corn and hay. This used a technology similar to the under-floor heating found in Roman baths. At the lowest level was a furnace

which heated the air in a chamber above. The corn itself was placed in a second chamber above the first and which was heated by air from below. The two chambers were connected by vents which could be opened or closed, allowing the farmer to regulate the heat in the kiln to ensure that the corn dried but did not burn.

In some parts of the empire, the Romans also used mills to grind their corn into flour, evidence of another mechanized, labour-saving process. There are remains of leats and water mills on Hadrian's Wall at Chesters, Willowford, and Haltwhistle Burn; animal power was used for milling in London and Cirencester, as it was in many parts of the empire on the continent. In most parts of Britain, however, mechanical mills seem to have been quite rare – or evidence for their use has not survived. The ancient method of grinding corn by hand with a stone quern probably continued in many places.

▼ FOUNDATIONS OF THE GRANARIES AT HOUSESTEADS ON HADRIAN'S WALL.

SILCHESTER, HAMPSHIRE

When it was excavated during the nineteenth and early twentieth centuries, Silchester revealed the complete plan of the Roman town of Calleva Atrebatum. The foundations of many buildings, including the forum, basilica, baths, and houses, were revealed. There were also four temples and a building with an apsidal (semi-circular) end, which may have been a church. All these remains were covered over after the excavation and so are not now visible.

Some features of the town can still be seen, however. Most impressive are the walls, which stand up to almost five metres high in places. Most of the facing stone has been removed, but the core of flint rubble, layers of flat slabs, and concrete remains to give the visitor a good idea of the solidity of the walls. Outside the walls are defensive earthworks from different stages in the history of the town, including some far beyond the walls, as if the inhabitants had at one point intended the town to be much larger.

Nearby, outside and to the east of the walls, is Silchester's amphitheatre. It survives as an earth bank that drops over five metres to the level of the arena. A stone retaining wall holds the bank in.

Most of the finds from Silchester are preserved in the Reading Museum, although there is also a small museum at the site.

▲ An aerial view of the Roman town of Silchester's walls.

THE ORIGINS OF TOWNS

Much of the food grown in the fields of Roman Britain was destined for the towns, many of which were entirely new settlements founded by the Romans, and which transformed the British landscape for good. The towns were centres of trade and commerce and home to an increasing proportion of the population, and as such they played a more and more vital part in the life of Roman Britain. Many of today's towns, from Exeter and Rochester in the south to Chester and Lancaster in the north, began life in the Roman period. Roman towns played, and still play, a huge part in the life of the island of Britain.

Towns grew up in Roman Britain for a variety of reasons. The first group to build after the invasion was the army, with its network of forts. In the second half of the first century, with much of England under Roman control, some military bases were being closed down and legionaries were being freed from service. Redundant bases, such as Colchester, Lincoln, and Gloucester, became towns, their fortifications, streets, and even some of their buildings put to new use to house and protect former soldiers. Once they were established, such settlements expanded beyond the bounds of the original fort to become important urban centres in their own right. These three towns (together, later, with York) became coloniae, high-status towns inhabited by Roman citizens.

▼ THE BATH HOUSE (TOP LEFT) AND FORUM (RIGHT) ARE THE MAIN STRUCTURES IN THIS RECONSTRUCTION OF ROMAN WROXETER.

Towns of slightly lower status, municipiae, were often 'promoted' from settlements that already existed. They numbered non-citizens among their inhabitants and could retain some local laws alongside Roman law. The clearest example of this type of town in Britain is Verulamium (St Albans).

It was not only the invaders who set up towns for 'their' people. The Britons were willing and eager to adopt Roman culture, to become 'Romanized', and the invaders themselves were keen for this to happen. They encouraged native tribal leaders to adopt Roman culture and comforts, to wear Roman clothes, and to educate their sons in the Roman manner. As part and parcel of this process, the British built new tribal capitals in the Roman style, often with the help of the invaders. These towns made up a third class of urban centre, the civitas capitals. Like the others, they were carefully planned and could become major towns. Examples include Silchester, Cirencester, Leicester, and Exeter. In the civitas capitals the locals were kept happy and comfortable, and felt that

they were becoming part of a privileged Roman elite. The Romans, meanwhile, kept their hands on a province that was content and less likely to rebel or cause other difficulties. They, and the rich Britons, could also make money from renting property in towns. But this form of business brought problems as well as profits. Cicero complained that two of his properties were in disrepair. 'Not only have the tenants left, but even the mice have quit,' he wrote.

There was another type of settlement, the vicus, which was a civilian community that grew up near a Roman fort. Forts attracted trade, especially if they were built at the intersection of two or more roads, so civilian settlements with markets or merchants' houses were often founded alongside forts. With a ready market for goods and services, such civilian settlements could prosper and survive the military bases that gave birth to them. Unlike the true towns, these vici were not planned, but they could be thriving, busy communities nonetheless.

▼ REMAINS OF A HYPOCAUST DOMINATE THIS VIEW OF THE SITE OF WROXETER.

VERULAMIUM, HERTFORDSHIRE

The Roman city of Verulamium was the third largest in Britain. Its site, still largely free of modern buildings, is near the present-day city of St Albans. The settlement began as the capital of the local British tribe, the Catuvellauni. When the Romans came they built a military base, but this quickly grew into a civilian town with a grid plan and wooden buildings. Subsequent rebuildings in the first and second centuries saw more and more construction in stone. There was further building work in the fourth century, and the city seems to have remained prosperous after the end of Roman rule.

Visitors to Verulamium can see the remains of the only surviving Roman theatre in Britain. This compact, round structure has quite a complex history and went through several rebuildings. Unlike an amphitheatre, it consisted of a raised stage, in front of which was a flat circular area called the orchestra, which was in fact an area for performance and dancing. Around the orchestra, tiered seating swept in a great arc. This theatre would probably have been used for pastimes such as bear-baiting as well as for dramatic performances.

There are various remains of shops and houses at Verulamium, of which many foundations are preserved. Finds from some of them, including fragments of mosaic and painted plaster from the walls, can be seen in the site museum. One notable remnant still in situ is the hypocaust, part of the pavement and under-floor heating system of a domestic bath house.

The basilica at Verulamium lies beneath St Michael's church, but the corner of the building can be seen marked out on the ground. Other remains of this city include parts of the defensive walls. These rise to three metres in places, and the foundations of one of the city's gates are marked out in flint on the ground. Beyond the walls is a deep defensive ditch.

TOWN PLANNING

By modern standards, Roman towns were not large. The biggest and most important of all was London, which became the provincial capital. London covered a site slightly smaller than the modern financial centre – roughly from a point slightly west of St Paul's Cathedral to the Tower, and from the River Thames to the line of modern Old Street. The total area was around 330 acres.

Others, such as Cirencester and St Albans (at 240 and 225 acres respectively) came near to London in size, but many were far smaller. Gloucester, for example, covered a mere 46 acres. As for their populations, London may have contained around 30,000 people; Gloucester might only have had 5,000 inhabitants.

Whether large or small, what were the distinctive features of a Roman town? The most fundamental was the plan: Roman towns, frequently built from scratch, were planned in a systematic way, using a grid pattern like a modern American city. The straight roads crossed at right-angles to create rectangular city blocks, known as insulae. On these rectangular sites stood the rectangular structures – houses, shops, and public buildings – that made up the typical Roman townscape.

This would have looked strikingly new in a Britain in which many houses were round and in which most settlements grew organically with little or nothing in the way of a master plan. Roman towns would have looked much more regimented and ordered than earlier British settlements.

The architectural style would also have been markedly different. However, we should not run away with the idea that Romano-British towns were full of elegant classical buildings, like the stone-built column-fronted temples that can be seen at continental sites and which fill books on Roman architecture. To begin with, most Roman buildings in Britain were of wood. When more permanent buildings were constructed, they were often of brick. Moreover very few Romano-British temples had classical fronts with columns – although the famous and important temple of Minerva at Bath and the temple of the imperial cult at Colchester were exceptions to this rule.

PUBLIC BUILDINGS

But the types of buildings in a Roman city were very different from what had gone before. At the centre of a Roman town was the forum, a central piazza, usually at the meeting place of two major roads, which acted as the heart of the town. Around three sides of the forum was a covered walkway or portico, supported by rows of columns. On the fourth side was the basilica, a large hall that acted as town hall and law court. The basilica was often the largest building in a town. London's basilica, the biggest of them all, was more than 500 feet long. The other sides of the forum usually contained shops, stalls, and eating-places. Above the shops were offices and storerooms, and market stalls were often put up in the portico and in the centre of the piazza.

So the forum was the town's centre of government and trade. Here there would be ironmongers and carpenters, butchers and bakers, sellers of glassware and leather goods. It was an important gathering point, a bustling space where fellow citizens could meet and exchange news, and the origin of the great public squares and courtyards that still adorn our cities.

Another important social centre in a Roman town was the bath house. For the Romans, bathing was a social event, not just a question of keeping clean. The public bath house in a Roman town was like a modern gym or sports club, a place where people went to bathe, exercise, and meet their friends. The well-to-do might even agree business deals there. The bath house was a large complex, with changing rooms, exercise areas, and various rooms for bathing (see page 121). Large cities had several bath houses, and they were some of the best-used buildings in town.

▼ THE CITY OF BATH, WITH ITS GREAT BATHING POOL.

Other important buildings stood nearby. These would often include a building called a mansio, which was rather like a hotel for those on official business in the town. The building contained a courtyard surrounded by rooms, together with stables, a bath house, and other public rooms. High-ranking soldiers, government officers, and couriers passing through the town would all stay at the mansio. One important purpose of a mansio was as a staging-post for the Roman postal service.

The town's temples, tall square buildings surrounded by a lower veranda or portico, would also be found near the centre. These were not large structures intended for congregational worship, but small buildings containing a shrine where people could leave offerings. Ceremonies involving larger numbers of people could be held out of doors in the temple precinct.

WROXETER, SHROPSHIRE

The town of Wroxeter began as a legionary fortress and was turned into the tribal capital of the Cornovii, hence its name Viroconium Cornoviorum. It was a big town, the fourth largest in Britain, and a large section of the site can still be seen because of the lack of later buildings.

The most prominent structure on the site is a tall section of wall now called the Old Work. It was a wall of a large hall, which was used as an exercise room next to the baths. The remains of the hypocaust system of the baths themselves can be seen in front of the Old Work. The different rooms of the bath complex can be made out, together with an open-air swimming pool, an unusual feature in Britain's cold climate.

Many other remains have been excavated at Wroxeter, including numerous houses, shops, and a very large house similar in plan to many country villas. These remains suggest that the town had a period of prosperity, and by the end of the second century it was also fortified. Second-century earthworks can still be seen around the site, and by the early third century there was also a stone wall. But the town seems to have declined in the third century, when the basilica, forum, and baths were partly demolished and timber buildings replaced some of those that had been knocked down.

HOUSES AND SHOPS

Most of the buildings in Roman towns were houses and shops, and the two functions were frequently combined in the same structure. For the most part, these were simple rectangular buildings, with a short street frontage. Looking out on to the street would be the shop, its front open to view during the day and closed with wooden shutters at night. Depending on the business, the shop might double as the workroom where the proprietor made, as well as sold, his pots, leatherware, or wooden products. Behind the shop was the family's living accommodation. Shops like this were originally built of wood, or of a timber frame with a clay infill. As time went on, and prosperity increased, wooden shops were often rebuilt in stone. If the shopkeeper owned his shop (rather than being a tenant or a slave who managed the shop for his owner), he would rebuild in stone when finances allowed.

In some streets there were larger houses, built for richer inhabitants. These houses could have two wings, on an L-shaped plan, or, in an even grander arrangement, could have three or four wings ranged around a courtyard. Houses like this were occupied by Roman citizens and Romanized Britons who had amassed considerable wealth. Such individuals had servants or slaves, and their houses included rooms for such staff. Heating came from open fires or braziers.

As time went on, and more of these large houses were rebuilt in stone or brick, the opportunity came to construct furnaces and hypocausts for under-floor heating. Other luxuries, such as mosaic floors or painted walls, might also be provided. The small courtyard gardens of these upper-class houses, containing flowers, herbs, and perhaps a central pool, were rare oases of greenery in the busy, dusty streets of a Roman town.

Although upper-class houses could be quite spacious, there was usually little room for expansion in the centre of a town, so if an owner wanted more room but didn't want to move, the only answer was to build upwards. As a result, many British houses had two storeys, and this in itself was an advance on what had been known before the Romans arrived. But Roman builders went even higher. We know from European sites, such as Ostia, the port of Rome, that the Romans could build quite tall buildings with shops on the ground floor and apartments above. One Roman document directs the reader to the seventh floor! Some British towns, too, may have had high-rise blocks, bringing a taste of the high-density living that we think of as typical of the modern city.

Another feature made some Roman houses different from what had gone before – glass windows. Ancient British houses did not have windows, just door openings which probably spent most of their time covered to keep out the cold. In the Roman world, on the other hand, glazed windows were available for those with enough money to pay for glass, which was still a luxury product.

The Romans did not invent glass – the Egyptians and Phoenicians before them had made glass vessels – but they did improve glass-making techniques and develop the process of glass blowing, which appeared in western Asia in Roman times. Even so, the Romans did not understand how to make glass perfectly transparent. Most of their glass is discoloured (often in an attractive way) by impurities in the ingredients. But Roman glass did let in some light and keep out the cold, and this was useful in a northern province like Britain.

Crammed together on small sites, the majority of Roman city houses lacked modern facilities such as kitchens and bathrooms. Native British houses of the same period were even simpler, of course – just a single room which had to accommodate a whole family as they cooked, ate, slept, and went about their daily business. For city-dwelling Romans jammed together in their wooden houses, cooking often posed a fire risk and as a result of these cramped conditions, many Romans ate take-away food from the local bar.

▼ THE TOMBSTONE OF REGINA, THE BRITISH WIFE (AND FORMERLY SLAVE) OF A MERCHANT CALLED BARATES, FROM PALMYRA. THE COUPLE ENDED UP LIVING NEAR HADRIAN'S WALL, AND REGINA'S TOMBSTONE IS AT SOUTH SHIELDS. THE BOTTOM LINE OF TEXT IS IN BARATES' NATIVE LANGUAGE, ARAMEIC.

Bars sold dishes such as hot breads, pastries, meats, and pies, a surprisingly modern selection. According to one first-century recipe, the Romans even made a dish like today's hamburger – a mixture of ground beef, salt, pine kernels, and a little wine, shaped together into a patty, fried, and eaten with bread – cheap, fast food for a Roman in a hurry.

With their ready supply of food and drink, such bars became lively gathering points for all. They were so popular that some emperors feared they might become the meeting-places for anti-government conspirators. Claudius is said to have tried to close them down, although he liked his food and said on another occasion, 'I ask you, who can live without a snack?'

MULTICULTURAL BRITAIN

Roman towns differed in one key way from previous settlements in Britain, and it is a way which makes them seem peculiarly modern: the Roman empire provided Britain's first multicultural society. Soldiers of the empire, especially auxiliaries, came from far and wide – Spain, North Africa, Gaul, Germany, and western Asia. The merchants who followed them could also come from far afield. Inscriptions record several wine merchants who came from or travelled to Gaul. Merchants also travelled to Britain from western Asia, and one of them, Salmanes, who was probably a Syrian, ended up at Auchendavy by the Antonine Wall. Cities such as London and Cirencester, Wroxeter and St Albans would have thronged with people from all over the empire, and when merchants from far-flung places arrived, all would have been eager for news of their homelands and of the places through which the others had travelled.

At times there would have been a babble of different languages in the forums of British towns as travellers met up with others from their part of the world. But for the most part, the merchants, officials, and soldiers from all over the empire communicated with each other in the standard language of the western empire – Latin.

The progress of town-building

It used to be thought that the Romans had built their towns rapidly, quite soon after the conquest. Because of a remark by Tacitus, the general Agricola, who was governor of Britain between AD 78 and 84, was thought to have built numerous towns in the province. In fact, archaeological evidence is revealing that many important town buildings were begun much later, during the second century. For example, forums at Leicester, Caistor-by-Norwich, Wroxeter, Exeter, and Caerwent are of a second-century date, along with many city bath houses and numerous amphitheatres. Many of these structures were built in towns that already existed, and sometimes the grid plan had to be altered to accommodate them. In some cases, the second-century building was a replacement of an earlier structure. There was a similar pattern in house-building: a lot of new construction as well as the extension and rebuilding of existing houses.

So the history of Roman city-building was long and complex. A city might be laid out, with its grid plan and some wooden buildings in place, during the first century. The following century, the city might be extended, and many of the public buildings added or replaced in stone when funds allowed. The third century saw less activity. In many parts of the empire, towns declined in the third century, but in Britain, which had many recent stone buildings, towns probably survived quite well. By the end of the third century some cities were beginning to expand again. The basilica and forum at Cirencester were altered, for example, and new shops were built at St Albans. By the middle of the fourth century there seems to have been a decline, with many buildings falling into disuse. But this did not mark the end of Romano-British towns, which continued to survive, if not to prosper, until the Romans left in the fifth century.

▼ A HOLE IN A MOSAIC PAVE-MENT AT VERULAMIUM SHOWS THE HYPOCAUST BENEATH.

THE WATER SUPPLY

Facilities such as public bath houses and lavatories needed one thing above all – a reliable supply of water. In continental Europe, the Romans went to great lengths to secure a decent water supply for their cities. Their aqueducts stretched miles across the countryside, and crossed deep valleys on huge arched stone structures that are still among the world's most famous feats of engineering. Distribution tanks and cisterns also played an important part in ensuring a continuous stream of running water.

Roman Britain had nothing on the scale of the vast aqueducts of France and Spain, but archaeologists have unearthed the remains of water-supply systems at many British sites. The longest was at Lincoln, where some thirty-two kilometres of earthenware supply pipes have been found. Other settlements, such as Colchester, Silchester, Cirencester, and Canterbury, had wooden pipes. Lead

▲ At the Roman lavatory at Housesteads the stone drainage channels are preserved.

pipes can be seen at Bath. Leicester, Dorchester, Wroxeter, and Exeter were supplied by leats. The example at Dorchester was a channel about a metre deep, following a winding twelve-mile course down a gentle gradient towards the city.

Most of these systems were relatively modest compared with the great European aqueducts. In most Romano-British towns it was probably only the baths and lavatories that had a continuous water supply. The reason why running water did not extend to other buildings was probably cost. After all, many British towns had to wait years to get public baths at all. There was a thirty-year gap between the building of the forum and the public bath house at Wroxeter; at Leicester, the gap was over fifty years. In addition, the

British climate, and the abundance of springs and streams, made building aqueducts less of a priority than it was in many drier places on the continent.

Alongside the baths there were often public lavatories, the stone seats of which have been preserved in Pompeii. Part of a stone seat has also been found at the Roman fort at Housesteads on Hadrian's Wall. Seats were arranged in a row over a stone drainage channel and water was flushed along the channel from tanks, in a similar way to a modern flush toilet. Sponges on sticks were used as lavatory paper. There were no separate cubicles in Roman public toilets. There was no modern concept of personal privacy, and it is likely that visiting the lavatories was almost as social an event as a trip to the nearby baths.

Where water was piped in, waste could be channelled out. Roman sewers, built of stone, deep underground, are engineering achievements as impressive as aqueducts. Stone sewers have been excavated at Lincoln, where they took water from the streets, and York, where they served the fortress baths. The York sewers are some five metres below the modern ground level. They were created by digging a trench, into which the stone base and sides of the sewer were built. The engineers then placed capstones on top and covered the whole with earth, fitting man-holes for inspection every so often. The sewers in York are more than a metre high, so could take a generous flow of waste water from the fortress baths which they served. It has been calculated that up to 70,000 gallons per day could have flowed through the system. This would have included waste from the latrines, which was swept along the drains by the force of the waste water from the baths. In addition to the waste, the sewers also carried away items lost in the baths, and so have become a rich hunting-ground for modern archaeologists. The York sewers have yielded jewellery, gaming counters, and animal bones – useful clues for archaeologists about the

▼ A SPONGE WAS USED INSTEAD OF TOILET PAPER.

clothes, pastimes, and eating habits of people two thousand years ago. Fragments of sponge have also been found in the York sewers, and these pieces contained the microscopic eggs of a parasite found in the human gut, evidence of the use of sponges as a form of lavatory paper in the latrines.

In case of fire

Roman towns consisted of close-built clusters of buildings, often made of wood. Apartments, shops, and bars where food was cooked nestled together. As a result, Roman towns could be prone to fire, and once a fire started it could spread at speed and with devastating results. Vitruvius said when a fire had started, houses could go up like torches. Fortunately, the Romans had an answer in a fire-fighting service equipped with an early form of fire engine.

Fire engines seem to have been invented among the Greek-speaking scholars of Alexandria in the third century BC and were developed some two hundred years later by the Alexandrian

▼ Adam Hart-Davis tests a reconstruction of a Roman fire engine with some modern-day fire fighters.

inventor Hero. Hero's fire engine consisted of a hand-powered pump with a rocker-arm connected to a pair of cylinders. When you pushed the rocker-arm, the cylinders forced water out of a tank and through a nozzle. The nozzle could be adjusted so that the water could be aimed in any direction. The device was mounted on a cart, which probably also held a reservoir of water.

We know from Roman writers that there was a dedicated fire brigade in Rome, which was made up of several hundred slaves. It was said that they would arrive at the scene of a fire and extort a heavy payment before setting to work. Nevertheless, they successfully prevented fires from spreading in the capital for hundreds of years. There were probably few fire brigades outside Rome itself, but the wooden remains of a pump have been found at the British site of Silchester, and it may just be that it was used for putting out fires.

A LASTING INFLUENCE

In an island that had been previously dominated by a farming economy, and whose people had lived in small, unplanned settlements, towns were one of the biggest innovations brought with the Roman conquest of Britain. Visually, with their straight, paved streets, multi-storey houses, and grand public buildings, they were unlike anything seen in Britain before. Socially, they were also revolutionary, creating centres of trade and craftsmanship, headquarters for local government, meeting-places for people from all over the province, and sometimes from all over the empire.

The towns of Roman Britain could not have existed without the wealth of the countryside – from the rich food supply provided by the farms to the mineral wealth from Britain's mining industry. It enabled the building of important urban centres that benefited the countryside too. They provided markets for agricultural produce and places where ideas and news could be exchanged. Although the towns declined after the Romans left Britain in the fifth century, their influence lived on. They became major centres in the Middle Ages and are still some of the most important cities on the map of Britain today.

CHAPTER 5

LIFE OF LUXURY

It was not only the Romans who benefited from the agricultural improvements that they brought to Britain. Increased productivity allowed native farmers to sell their surplus grain and meat at a profit, so that many grew rich and aspired to a lifestyle like that of their conquerors. In a word, they became Romanized. As Roman culture became well established in Britain and the permanence of Roman rule seemed assured, some of these Romanized Britons began to live lives of luxury. That is not to say that the Britons were not capable of sophistication already. Their metalwork, from engraved bronze mirrors to beautifully crafted swords, showed that they had highly developed arts and crafts; the word 'barbarian' is a misnomer for these people.

◀ THE GREAT MOSAIC AT LULLINGSTONE ROMAN VILLA: IN THE CENTRE OF THE MAIN ROOM BELLEROPHON RIDES THE WINGED HORSE PEGASUS; THE APSE MOSAIC SHOWS EUROPA AND THE BULL.

Nevertheless, the Britons saw much that was new and attractive in the Roman way of life. They wanted the lavish houses, rich diet, and fashionable clothes of the wealthy Romans. They aspired to educate their sons in Roman ways and Roman culture. Evidence of this life of luxury is to be found all over southern England, especially south and east of a line following roughly the Rivers Severn and Trent. Above all, this is the heartland of the villas – large, elegant, sometimes palatial houses dotted around the British countryside. Villas were laid out spaciously, equipped with the latest heating and bathing facilities, and decorated in the Roman fashion. For the Britons, they represented a quantum leap in luxury.

THE VILLA

Most Roman villas were first and foremost farms, but farms that could also be large and comfortable country houses. Villas come in all sorts of shapes and sizes. Back in the 1960s, the influential historians of Roman Britain, R. G. Collingwood and I. A. Richmond, described four main types of Roman villa in England. Simplest of all was the cottage house, a small building, often timber framed, built in a single block with a few interconnecting rooms. Then there was the corridor house, often larger, in which the rooms were linked by a long passage, affording more privacy. Bigger and more elaborate still were the courtyard houses, in which the buildings were arranged around two or more sides of a rectangular court. Finally there were the aisled buildings, designed rather like a church, with a central space (the nave) flanked by two aisles, which could be used either for residential accommodation, as farm buildings, or as a combination of the two.

These were not standard designs, reproduced identically like Roman forts. They were basic patterns which builders varied endlessly, so that every Roman villa is different. Villas often grew over the centuries, starting as cottage houses, acquiring corridors, and growing into courtyard complexes as the prosperity of the owner increased. Some also suffered a decline, with living accommodation turned over to agricultural use towards the end of the Roman period.

A large villa incorporated a variety of rooms and buildings, both residential and working. The living accommodation might include a big reception or dining-room, a kitchen, and a bath complex. There would also be numerous smaller rooms, perhaps bedrooms, although it is usually difficult for archaeologists to tell exactly what they were used for. Sometimes there were two suites of rooms, suggesting that the villa may have been occupied by two families at once.

There would also be farm buildings, such as barns, corn driers, and rooms for storage. There might also be offices, for there would be plenty of administration to do on a large villa estate, and some villas were also the headquarters for industrial activity, such as pottery, metalworking, or quarrying.

Roman villas could be houses of great sophistication and luxury. Even the simplest villas were a far cry from anything built by the native Britons. The most basic of features, such as separate rooms and corridors, gave a sense of privacy quite unknown in the simple, one-room houses of the Celts. Separate rooms also allowed villa-dwellers to partition off one domestic function from another, so that food, for example, could be prepared in one place and eaten in another, and work activities such as grinding corn could be carried out in a quite separate place from the house.

But the luxury of the villa could go much further than this.

▼ AN ARTIST'S RECONSTRUCTION OF LULLINGSTONE ROMAN VILLA: THE BATH SUITE IS BOTTOM LEFT.

Large, high-status villas had beautifully decorated rooms with mosaic floors and painted walls. Some even had glazed windows. They were comfortable and well furnished, warm and free from draughts. Villas like these were possible only with new technologies imported by the Romans and enthusiastically taken up by Romanized Britons.

LULLINGSTONE, KENT

The villa at Lullingstone is a good example of how an archaeological site can reveal different episodes in the lives of its various occupants. A simple house, with one range of rooms and a corridor, was built here in the late first century. In the late second century, the villa was extended, with bath suites at one end and a shrine at the other. The expansion implies a family of some standing, and they owned marble busts of some of their ancestors. But quite suddenly their fortunes seem to have changed. In around AD 200 they left the villa in a hurry, leaving many of their possessions behind them, including the marble busts.

Towards the end of the third century, new owners arrived. They built a granary, restored the baths, and built a long room on the site of the shrine. In the fourth century the family converted to Christianity and constructed what was probably a chapel in the villa. They also filled in the baths and pulled down the granary. The next century there was a fire, and the villa was finally abandoned.

Today's visitors can see evidence of all these phases of occupation in a series of ruins protected by a modern roof. Highlights include mosaics of Europa and the bull, and Bellerophon, riding the winged horse Pegasus, killing the monstrous Chimera. Some key finds, such as the marble busts and wall plaster with Christian symbols, are in the British Museum, but reproductions are shown at the villa itself.

The Bellerophon mosaic dates from the villa's Christian period, and it has been suggested that here the classical myth has a Christian meaning, with the hero's killing of the monster symbolizing the victory of good over evil.

▼ REMAINS OF THE HOT ROOM, HOT BATH, AND FURNACE, LULLINGSTONE.

THE ART OF THE MOSAIC

A favourite form of decoration was the mosaic pavement. The art of mosaic was unknown in England before the Romans. It involved cutting tiny pieces, called tesserae, from different coloured stones, arranging them to form patterns, and fixing them in place on a bed of mortar. The bed would be carefully prepared to give a solid foundation to the floor, with a base of gravel followed by layers of mortar, getting gradually smoother towards the top. It was not easy to lay tesserae on this surface, because it involved placing the pieces of stone on the damp mortar, and on a floor of any size the mosaic-maker would have to walk and kneel on the floor itself as he worked.

There were various ways around this problem. One method was to work in sections, laying the tesserae on one patch of wet mortar before moving on to the next section. Usually, the mosaic-maker began in the centre of the floor, moving gradually outwards. Work would have to proceed quickly, before the mortar dried. To keep the work square while working at speed, mosaic-makers used a variety of templates, together with tools such as set-squares. This method was best for simple designs, such as the repeating patterns that were often used around the edge of a mosaic pavement.

▾ ZEUS, DISGUISED AS AN EAGLE, ABDUCTS THE YOUTH GANYMEDE, IN A MOSAIC AT BIGNOR VILLA.

Another method used a sort of prefabrication technique. The tesserae were first stuck to a sheet of linen with a water-soluble glue. The gaps between the tesserae were then 'grouted' with a fine mortar mix, and the resulting panel was protected between two boards. Next the mosaic-worker scratched guidelines into the damp mortar on the floor to indicate where the panel should be placed. The panel could then be laid, cloth upwards, on to the damp cement, and the lower board slid away. When the mortar had dried, the mosaic-maker could remove the linen by dissolving the glue. One advantage of the linen method was that a design could be sketched out on the cloth before the tesserae were stuck down. This made the technique well suited to the more complex designs which were often placed at the centres of mosaic floors.

Mosaic-makers often used standard designs for villa floors. Most of these probably came directly from the continent, and craftsmen may even have brought pattern-books with them which they then copied, in the same way that the builders of eighteenth-century houses used such books to design features such as cornices and door cases. As time went by, specialist mosaic workshops were set up in Romano-British towns, and it is possible to trace the style and subject matter of the mosaics produced at these different centres. By the second century, mosaics had become quite widespread in both villas and large town houses, creating a style of interior decoration quite alien to anything seen in Britain before the Romans arrived.

Many mosaics survive, in whole or in part, at villa sites in Britain. Major villas such as Lullingstone and Bignor, and the palace at Fishbourne have excellent examples. One of the most famous is the huge one at Woodchester, Gloucestershire, which is covered from view although a reproduction of the mosaic restored to its full glory is often displayed. Its subject, Orpheus, the musician of classical mythology, was a popular one. The villa at Littlecote also has an Orpheus mosaic which adorns a room that seems to have been used for some form of ceremony. In this mosaic, Orpheus' companions are Venus, goddess of love, spring, and rebirth, and panthers, creatures who traditionally accompanied Bacchus, the god of wine and revelry. With such decorations, it is likely that the ceremonies held in the room involved feasting, drinking, and revelry. Major reception rooms in villas, particularly dining-rooms, often had mosaics with similar subject matter.

CHEDWORTH, GLOUCESTERSHIRE

This is one of Britain's best preserved villas. It is sited in the Cotswolds, near a spring and a few kilometres away from an important Roman road, the Fosse Way. The villa was built in a series of stages between the second and fourth centuries, beginning as a cluster of separate buildings, which were finally connected by a corridor or veranda to form a courtyard enclosing a formal garden. There was also another courtyard, consisting of farm buildings.

By the fourth century the villa had a fine dining-room with painted plaster walls. The main part of this room had a mosaic floor with a geometric design, but the anteroom has a floor with figurative mosaics. Much of this remains today, including figures representing spring, summer, and autumn (winter has been destroyed).

The villa features two bath suites, one for damp heat, the other for dry-heat sauna-type bathing. The former is well preserved, with mosaic floors, hypocausts, and furnace all visible.

Many other rooms can be seen. They include the service wing, which has a kitchen with the base of a circular oven, a latrine with sewer, and a room now known as the steward's office, where many coins were found.

To the north-east was a shrine with an eight-sided pool at the site of the villa's spring. On the paving stones here are Christian symbols, suggesting that the residents converted to Christianity at some point during the villa's occupation.

▼ THE FIGURE OF SPRING FROM THE DINING-ROOM MOSAIC AT CHEDWORTH VILLA.

FRESCOES

Villas frequently had beautifully painted walls. Fragments of painted plaster have been found on many villa sites, and some show painting of great skill and beauty. From the pieces that have been retrieved, it seems that plastered and painted walls were very common in Roman Britain. In many cases, the colour scheme was quite simple, with walls painted in a single plain colour or in coloured panels. A more elaborate scheme could be achieved with 'architectural' motifs, in which features such as columns, bases, and capitals were imitated in paint. Sometimes in this type of decoration, shading and perspective were used cleverly in a trompe l'oeil technique. A good example of this style was found at the so-called 'Painted House' at Dover. Here the decorative scheme featured a row of columns framing a series of panels with borders of red, yellow, and orange. Inside the panels were painted naturalistic details such as branches, palm fronds, and plant tendrils. Architectural decorations could continue up into the ceiling, where painted squares could imitate the panelled, or coffered, ceilings popular with Roman architects.

More elaborate still were walls on which there were quite ambitious figurative paintings. Famous examples include a fine portrait head found in pieces at Sparsholt, Hampshire, and mythological subjects such as the cupid found at Southwell. Gladiators, theatrical masks, and heads of gorgons were other motifs from Roman culture which seem to have been prized by Romanized Britons when they decorated their luxurious houses in both town and country.

The technique used for these wall paintings was called fresco, a method that involves applying paint to the plaster while it is still wet. The advantage of fresco technique is that the paint becomes part of the surface of the plaster. As it dries, evaporating water comes to the surface, bringing with it lime from the plaster. This reacts to produce a protective clear layer of calcium carbonate over the painting.

Fresco painting requires careful preparation of the surface before the artist can begin. Roman workers built up the plaster in several layers. They began with a relatively coarse mortar-like rendering, to create a fairly uniform surface. This was followed with further layers, getting finer and finer, until the plasterer finished with a layer of the finest plaster, in which marble dust or powdered calcite was mixed to give a white finish.

▼ FRAGMENTS OF PAINTED WALL PLASTER FROM LULLINGSTONE SHOW A MAN IN THE POSITION USED BY EARLY CHRISTIANS FOR PRAYER.

When applying the final layer, the plasterer had to bear in mind how much of the wall the painter could cover in one work session. Dividing the wall up into panels provided a good way of disguising the joins between separate sessions of painting. To apply the colour, the painters used mostly earth pigments – yellow and red ochres, green earth, and chalk for white. There were also some mineral pigments, but these were much rarer, especially in far-flung provinces such as Britain. Charcoal made a serviceable black.

Even with these simple resources, Roman artists could produce impressive effects. Their colours were rich, their architectural decorations could be elegant, and some of their figure work has a freedom and vibrancy all its own. At their best, they could produce decoration that was more sophisticated than modern paint and wallpaper, and was certainly very different from the dark walls of native British houses.

THE BATHS

A typical villa had its own bath complex, for the use of the owner and his family. Like the great public baths in Roman towns, these were large, had several rooms, and were intended for relaxation as well as for hygiene. The writer Seneca, who lived above a public bath in Rome, wrote a letter in which he comments about all the noises he heard there. He talks about the cries of people jumping into the plunge pools, the shouting of sausage sellers, and the screams of those having their armpits plucked. Similar mingled cries of pain and pleasure – minus the sausage sellers, of course – would no doubt have come from the bath house in a country villa.

Although many Romans varied their practice according to their mood and the amount of time at their disposal, the usual idea was to go through the baths in a particular sequence. Users would arrive in the first room, which was an unheated changing room (the *apodyterium*) where they would remove their clothes. Next they would spend some time in a warm room (or *tepidarium*) before carrying on into the hot room (or *caldarium*). The heat, which could be quite intense, opened the pores and made the bather sweat, and a slave would remove both perspiration and dirt with a curved metal scraper called a strigil. Sometimes the slave also massaged in olive oil. The bather then returned through the warm and cold rooms, ending with a cold plunge and a good towelling down. There were many variations on the sequence, and some villas had bath suites with extra warm rooms or more than one plunge bath, according to the owner's preferences.

Bath suites had to have quite elaborate heating systems. The heat was provided by a furnace built underground. As well as heating the water tank that supplied the hot plunge bath, this warmed the under-floor space or hypocaust, which extended beneath the hot and warm rooms. Heat would pass up through the floor to heat the rooms above. In addition, the hot rooms could be lined with hollow tiles which acted as flues, carrying warm air up the walls and inside the vaulted roofs, again sending more heat into the rooms. With an efficient hypocaust system, a stifling heat could build up inside the room. The floor could get so hot that the bathers had to wear special wooden sandals to protect their feet.

▼ VIEW OF A RECONSTRUCTED HYPOCAUST AT WALLSEND, SHOWING THE BRICK PILLARS THAT HOLD UP THE FLOOR.

There were bath complexes all over the Roman empire. One of the most famous of all was at the city of Bath, where the Great Bath formed the heart of a religious complex. This was rather unusual, in that it was a bath in which people swam. Typical of the elaborate multi-room bath house seen at many Roman sites is the military bath house at the fort of Chesters on Hadrian's Wall. Here one can still see the walls of the changing room, which rise to almost two metres in height in places. One of these walls has a row of seven niches, which would probably have had wooden doors to form lockers for bathers' clothes. Originally, there would probably have been another row of niches above. Beyond stretched a suite of rooms – cold and hot, moist and dry – which the user could visit in various different sequences. Many villas had a much smaller bath suite, but there would still have been this variety of rooms and potential sequences.

▲ THE INTERIOR OF THE RECONSTRUCTED BATH HOUSE AT WALLSEND BASED ON THE REMAINS OF CHESTERS.

PERSONAL GROOMING

Bathing was just one aspect of the Roman regard for personal hygiene and appearance. Grooming and cosmetics were important too. The historian Tacitus says that by the time of the Romanizing governor Agricola's second year in Britain, the toga was seen everywhere – clearly Britons were eager to take up Roman fashions. The same went for grooming and cosmetics. A favourite accessory for a Roman was a 'pocket set' consisting of tweezers, nail cleaner, nail file, toothpick, and ear scoop, all made of bronze and suspended on a metal loop like a large key ring which could be attached to one's belt. The tweezers were particularly important because the Romans hated body hair. Pliny mentions a depilatory cream made of the blood of a she-goat mixed with dried viper's blood. Many must have tried preparations like this in the hope of removing their body hair painlessly, but in the end most Romans had to grit their teeth and use their tweezers.

The Romans also used mirrors. They did not introduce the idea to Britain, for the Celts had polished metal mirrors which could be objects of beauty in their own right. But the Romans, with their glass-making technology, did produce the first glass mirrors to have survived, probably made during the third century. According to Pliny, the Romans got this idea from the Phoenicians, who were among the ancient world's most expert glass-workers.

The Romans were great users of cosmetics. Again, this practice was not new to Britain, but the Romans brought with them a whole repertoire of beauty treatments. Fashionable Roman women made up carefully in three stages. The face was whitened all over, using either poisonous white lead or the safer chalk. The eyes were made up in contrasting black. There were several black pigments – black antimony mixed with fat, soot with olive oil, burned rose petals, or even squashed flies. Finally rouge, generally in the form of red earth, was applied to the cheeks.

▼ RECONSTRUCTED ROMAN JEWELLERY MADE OF BRONZE, GOLD, AND SEMI-PRECIOUS STONES.

These cosmetics were expensive and were usually the preserve of the rich. The whitened complexion was designed to make the upper classes stand out from their poorer neighbours. A natural, sun-tanned face was a sign that you spent your days toiling in the fields. A pale face, in contrast, showed that you did not have to work and could spend most of your time indoors. Rich Roman women also used perfumes. These ranged from expensive ones

like myrrh mixed with spices, through to the more popular perfumes made with rose petals. The Romans looked after their teeth with a cleaning preparation made from burned eggshells, and whitened them with powdered pumice stone.

Many Roman cosmetics were damaging to the health, unlike one fashion – the use of wigs by women. This was a trend which became quite widespread among higher-ranking women, inspired by the wives of emperors. Women would see statues or coins bearing the image of the new empress and immediately wanted to imitate the first lady's hair style. This notion of fashion, with new ideas spreading across great distances as women copied images circulated via the coinage, was another aspect of life brought to Britain by the Romans. Hair of many different colours and styles was available to the Romans from all over their large empire. Some men also wore wigs, and on at least one occasion this fact had political implications. The emperor Caracalla, for example, donned a blond wig cut in the local style, together with local dress, when he visited Germany in AD 214.

Although most women now no longer regularly wear a wig, other aspects of Roman grooming have lasted well. Facial make-up using the three elements of foundation, mascara, and rouge is still popular, even if today the stark blacks and pallid whites of Roman cosmetics are seldom used.

▲ MAKE-UP COULD BE MIXED ON SHELLS OR SLATE PALETTES AND STORED IN WOODEN BOXES.

ENTERTAINING ROOMS

As we have seen, Roman houses were rectangular and contained rectangular rooms, in contrast to the round, single-roomed houses of the native Britons. But the more the Romans built in brick and stone, the more they used these materials to create interesting variations on room shapes.

It is not difficult for a skilled worker to build a curved wall of stone or brick, and any imperfections in the surface can easily be smoothed over with plaster. By the time they came to Britain, the Romans already had several centuries of experience in creating rooms with curved walls – circular rooms, and rooms with semi-circular or apsidal ends, for example. The Stabian Baths at Pompeii, dating to the second century BC, already had a circular cold room and a hot room with an apse.

In the more elaborate British villas and their bath suites, builders also began to experiment with different room shapes, transforming interior space in the process. Some of the most notable examples of this are dining-rooms. The Roman dining-room was called the triclinium, which means a room with three couches. These couches, arranged in a semicircle, were where the host and guests ate and were entertained. In Britain it may also have been the room in which workers and clients came to greet the householder in the morning ritual called the salutatio.

▼ AN ARTIST'S IMPRESSION OF THE INTERIOR AT LULLINGSTONE HAS A SEMICIRCULAR DINING-ROOM WITH COUCHES AND LOW TABLE.

The triclinium was thus the most important reception room in a villa. It often had an elaborate mosaic floor and finely painted walls. In some of the larger villas the room was semicircular in shape, mirroring the arrangement of the couches; alternatively it could be a rectangular room with an apsidal end. By the third century, the Roman fashion for an apsidal room with a semicircular dining couch had also spread to England. Large villas, such as those at Box, Bignor, and Lullingstone, had apsidal reception rooms. In some places there were even more elaborate designs, including a rectangular room with apses on three of its sides at Littlecote, Wiltshire, and an octagonal reception room at Great Witcombe, Gloucestershire. These rooms were often located in a central position in the villa, confirming their status as the most important room in the house.

All these rooms show how eager well-to-do Britons were to adopt Roman fashions, both in the architecture of their homes and presumably also in the way in which these rooms were used. Combined with mosaic decoration incorporating scenes from Roman mythology, they gave an effect of luxury. As the owner and his guests lounged on their dining couches in these elegant surroundings, they displayed a sophistication that could have been recognized by people from all over the empire.

FISHBOURNE, WEST SUSSEX

Well sited on the Sussex coast next to what was in Roman times a sheltered natural harbour, Fishbourne is the largest of all Romano-British houses, a palace rather than a villa. It was built on the site of earlier structures – a wooden military building put up soon after the conquest and a building, probably a house, erected in the time of Nero. The palace was built in the late 70s, after most of the earlier structures had been demolished.

Thought to be the residence of the local tribal king, Fishbourne was highly luxurious. The main rooms were arranged around a rectangular courtyard, and most of them had mosaic floors and painted walls. Some of the walls were even lined with panels of imported marble, a most unusual feature in Britain. Another rare feature was the use of mouldings of stucco. All these aspects point to the fact that the palace must have been constructed by a large number of skilled workers, many perhaps coming from Rome itself, at vast expense. Fishbourne must have been one of the wonders of Roman Britain.

Visitors to the palace entered through a hall lined with pillars and containing an ornamental pool. From this entrance in the east wing, they could go along the arcaded walkway that gave access to the whole courtyard, admiring the formal garden in the middle. Also in the east wing were two groups of small rooms around little courtyards, perhaps used for guest accommodation.

The west wing was the official area of the palace. It was dominated by a large room with an apse, probably an audience chamber, where the king received visitors. The south wing contained the owner's private apartments; these are now buried beneath modern buildings and a road. In the north wing were guest apartments arranged around two smaller courtyards. These rooms were lavishly decorated and had mosaic floors.

The palace would have been much larger than the three wings and courtyard visible today. As well as the vanished south wing, there would also have been service rooms and slaves' quarters, the whole creating a huge complex.

GREEN SPACES

Another feature of more luxurious Roman houses was the garden. In Rome itself, and in well-preserved Roman cities such as Pompeii, the houses of the well-to-do often had two outside spaces. Visitors coming in from the street would pass through an entrance passage into a central circulating space called the atrium. This was like a pillared courtyard, with a central area that was open to the sky. Beyond this was another courtyard, containing a garden. Whereas the atrium was the working heart of the home, where the man of the house welcomed guests and did business, the garden courtyard was the place of pleasure and leisure, filled with beautiful plants, classical statuary, and gently trickling fountains, and bordered by rooms such as the triclinium, where guests were entertained.

In Britain, on the edge of the empire, town houses of this size and complexity were probably rare, but the idea of the garden, the green space that could be both elegant and relaxing, was adopted by the Romano-British in their villas. The Romans introduced Britain to the idea of an ornamental space, with statues, trellises, fountains, and fishponds, where plants were grown for their beauty just as much as for their usefulness.

Perhaps the grandest of all Romano-British gardens was the one at Fishbourne, the palace which was probably occupied by Togidubnus, a client king who was made a Roman citizen in the time of Claudius. Togidubnus governed the local area of southern England where his palace was situated. This house was vast, with the main rooms arranged around a huge courtyard more than ninety metres across. And in the courtyard was a notable formal garden.

The great space was divided into two sections by a broad, hedge-lined path. Much of the space was probably laid to lawn, but there were also trees, arranged to enhance the views from important rooms in the palace. In addition, parts of the garden would have been adorned with plants popular in Roman times, such as roses, lilies, and acanthus. Fountains and basins, supplied by a network of underground pipes, completed the picture. In addition, the palace boasted an even bigger garden on an artificial terrace to the south. This was designed as a more natural landscape garden, with a stream, a pond, trees, and shrubs arranged informally.

Fishbourne is unique, a palace truly fit for a king on a huge ten-acre site. Other Romanized Britons had to make do with more compact villas in smaller grounds, but many of them would have had gardens too, for almost as much as bath houses and elegant interior decoration, they were part of the Roman way of life. Indeed they were a way of Romanizing the very land and landscape that people found around them, of bringing the literal roots and branches of the empire to its most far-flung outpost.

DELICACIES OF THE TABLE

Another way in which Britons could become Romanized was in their diet. For ordinary Romans, food was very basic. The staple diet of Rome was wheat, often eaten in the form of a porridge. The addition of herbs, vegetables, mushrooms, fish, or meat if it was available, gave the porridge some taste. But since many Roman cooks were slaves who had little experience or training in cookery, the result was often bland. The Roman poet Martial yearned for a cook who had the educated taste of his master: 'I would not have his palate to be that of a slave, a cook ought to have his master's taste.' The satirist Juvenal points out how the best food might be kept for the head of the household. A slave hands out the bread 'although it's so hard you can scarcely break it, mouldy bits of hardened dough that crack your teeth while stopping you bite them. But the master has a fresh, snow-white loaf made from the best flour specially reserved for him.' As in all historical periods, standards of food could vary widely.

The day for Romans began with breakfast, jentaculum. This traditionally consisted of biscuits or bread seasoned with salt, honey, dates, or olives. The working day followed, and it was not interrupted with a major meal. The main meal of the day, known as cena, followed when the work was over, at around 3 p.m. in summer, earlier in winter. This was when the porridge was served. There might also be a light supper, called vesperna, in the evening.

This was a regime of plain, uninspiring food. For rich Romans on special occasions, however, there was more variety. There are famous stories of Roman banquets featuring exotic or outlandish foods – larks' tongues, dormice, ostriches, mice cooked in honey, and so on. The Roman writer Petronius, in his novel the *Satyricon*, describes a banquet of memorable excess, served up by the rich merchant Trimalchio. At the feast Trimalchio presents dishes such as a sow stuffed with live thrushes and a hare fitted with wings in imitation of Pegasus, the mythical flying horse.

Tales like this relate the excesses of emperors and high-ranking pleasure-seekers in Rome, not the everyday taste of Romanized Britons. But their meals could be lavish too. A dinner party could begin with a starter course consisting of salads, eggs, oysters, sardines, and snails, a Roman introduction to Britain. After a drink of wine sweetened with honey, the main dishes arrived, and there could be six or seven of these – fish and sea-food, meats such as boar, venison, lamb, pork, hare, or dormouse, poultry of all kinds from chicken and geese to thrushes and peacocks. Finally came a dessert featuring fruit and cakes sweetened with honey.

This three-part format, the ancestor of our three-course meal, was another Roman introduction.

Rich meals like this would not have been served every day, although they demonstrate the Romans' ability to cook a vast range of foods. But villa-owners who were prepared to build elegant, Roman-style dining-rooms to entertain their guests would have wanted to serve elaborate meals in them, with more than a hint of the excesses of the capital. This is how they would have impressed friends and business associates. They might even have drawn on the work of the Roman writer Apicius, the great gourmet who wrote the recipe book *De Re Coquinaria*. Apicius recorded a variety of recipes under different headings. Meat (pork, venison, mutton, veal, lamb, kid, rabbit, and hare) and seafood (oysters, crabs, lobsters, mussels, sardines, tuna, skate, squid, and octopus) are covered extensively. There are also some exceptionally rich recipes including tripe, truffles, snails, mushrooms, lungs, and cakes. Altogether, the book provides a fascinating account of the sort of meals that Romans aspired to, even if they did not often sit down to some of Apicius' more outlandish delicacies, such as lungs or pigs' testicles.

WINE AND OIL

Although Britain was a rich place agriculturally, two of the Romans' most important crops did not grow there – the grape and the olive. These were such a key part of their diet, especially in the form of wine and olive oil, that it is hard to see how the Romans could have done without them for long. It seems that they did not need to, since wine was being imported from southern Italy into Britain in the first century BC, well before the Roman invasion.

After the Romans arrived, the flow of wine continued. Finds of amphorae at British sites suggest that the drink was coming in from Spain as well as from Italy. The Britons probably liked a drink just as much as the next people. Pliny reports the enthusiasm of the Gauls for wine, and the people of Britain may have been similar:

▼ THIS BRONZE FLAGON WAS FOUND AT LULLINGSTONE.

'their desire makes them drink it greedily and when they become drunk they fall into a stupor or into a maniacal disposition'.

During the reign of Septimus Severus (193–211), civil wars disrupted the wine trade in Spain, and suppliers from elsewhere in the empire, notably Germany and France, took over. Was wine produced in Britain itself? It certainly was, although it is difficult to know whether it was made in quantity. In the late third century, when the economy in Gaul and Britain was suffering a decline, the emperor Probus changed the law, abolishing restrictions on vineyards in these areas. Given Britain's climate, however, the province is unlikely ever to have been a major producer like the areas further south.

As in so many fields, the Romans turned their technological resources to the wine industry. Grapes need to be pressed to extract the juice. The traditional way to do this is by treading, but many wine producers preferred to follow this with mechanical pressing to squeeze out more of the juice. This second stage had been done with a lever-operated press, but the Greeks introduced a screw press, which they also used to squeeze the oil out of olives.

Making a screw press was more difficult than it looks. This is because, as well as cutting a large thread on the vertical screw of the machine, the engineer also has to cut an *internal* thread for the screw to engage with. In other words, the device works like a giant nut and bolt. It must have required great skill and care in the cutting of the threads to produce a mechanism that worked smoothly and efficiently.

The Romans could devote as much thought to the layout of the winery as to the machine itself. Palladius, the Roman writer of the treatise *On Agriculture*, describes how the building should be arranged. He begins with the position, and his account certainly gives us a

▼ USING A LATHE TO CUT THE THREAD ON THE SCREW.

sample of the smells of the Roman world: 'We should have a winery that faces north, is cool or as dim as possible, and at a distance from the baths, stables, oven, dung hills, cisterns, standing water, and other places that give off a terrible stench.' Palladius continues with a description of the building, which he suggests should be like a basilica, but with the treading floor on a higher level than the tanks, so that the grape juice can flow directly into storage tanks or barrels.

CENTRES OF WEALTH

Villas, with their rich farmland and luxurious lifestyle, obviously made attractive homes for the upper classes of Roman Britain, but historians are not sure exactly how these villas fitted into the British economy. The picture is muddled, partly because the term 'villa' is used for everything from small farmhouses to a vast palace like Fishbourne, but most villas were centres of farming. Finds of numerous writing styli at some sites point to the fact that they were also administrative centres, where the produce of the farm would be recorded, together with the details of sales, profits, and the amount owed in tax. Villas were places of luxury, and it is easy to imagine them as centres of a life of ease, where a leisured class could wander through formal gardens and linger in the bath house or triclinium, but they were also places of work, vital to the production of all food needed for Britain's growing population – from administrators to peasants, soldiers to slaves. The villas were probably central to the economic wellbeing of Roman Britain.

▲ THE RECONSTRUCTED PRESS USED IN THE WINE-MAKING PROCESS.

CHAPTER 6

AHEAD OF THEIR TIME

The Romans proved highly effective rulers of Britain, and brought with them many innovations, from bath houses and roads to advanced weapons and machines, that transformed the British scene. These new inventions were far in advance of what had gone before in Britain – and in many cases they were more sophisticated than what came after the Romans left. The Romans must have seemed ahead of their time.

Many people had a good life surrounded by the innovations that the Romans brought, and upper-class Romanized Britons grew rich under Roman rule. Their villas, and the lavish art and decoration that they left behind, are testimony to this. The towns, Britain's first sizeable planned settlements, were also the products of prosperity, centres of

◀ A ROMAN MOSAIC IN SICILY DEPICTS A GIRL WEARING A BIKINI. SIMILAR BIKINI BOTTOMS, MADE OF LEATHER, HAVE BEEN FOUND AMONG THE REMAINS OF ROMAN LONDON.

trade and local government that were quite unlike what had gone before. And the Romans ruled Britain for around 400 years, a vast stretch of time when we consider that 400 years ago in Britain, Elizabeth I was on the throne. By any standards, it was a formidable achievement.

Perhaps if the Romans had continued to innovate using technology to adapt to the changing scene in their provinces, they would have held on to their empire for even longer. But they could not repeat the explosion of innovation that they brought at the first century

In any case the Romans were not as strong as they seemed. As we have seen, they did not rule the whole island. Although they were quick to conquer the south-east, they took much longer to extend their dominance into the north and west, and they were never able to rule in Scotland for any length of time, as their experience on Hadrian's Wall showed.

BIGNOR, WEST SUSSEX

Growing slowly over the years on the site of a first-century farm, Bignor is a major villa site in south-east England that was at its most prosperous towards the end of the Roman period. Its first stone buildings were constructed in the first half of the third century, but the villa's true heyday was in the fourth century, by which time its buildings stretched around a rectangular courtyard. There was one bath suite, in the south wing, and the main reception rooms were in the west wing.

Many of the rooms at Bignor had hypocausts and mosaic floors. The mosaics are Bignor's most remarkable features. Even the corridor, originally 230 feet long, had a mosaic with a geometrical pattern. About 80 feet of this corridor mosaic is still preserved. Another mosaic of high quality shows an eagle carrying Ganymede, the boy who became cup-bearer to the king of the gods on Mount Olympus. Other notable mosaic subjects are Medusa and the seasons, including a fine portrayal of the head of Winter, dressed in a cloak and hood. A third high-quality pavement shows Venus, portrayed with a halo and surrounded by birds and other decorations. She is accompanied by Cupids portrayed as gladiators.

THREATS TO SECURITY

▶ ONE OF THE MANY LATE-ROMAN MOSAICS AT BIGNOR VILLA.

In spite of the strength of the Roman army, the sophistication of their weapons, and their network of forts and roads, Roman rule in

Britain was threatened from time to time, both from resistance in Scotland and from attacks from Northern Europe. In the early third century, for example, the Romans, under the emperor Septimus Severus, tried once more to subdue Scotland. Severus, who was born in the far south of the empire in North Africa, arrived in Britain in 208, and the following year saw him in territory that must have seemed completely alien to him, on campaign against the locals in Scotland. His legions scored some victories and he made the Caledonian leaders come to terms, but there was another uprising and in the winter of 210–211 the emperor once again prepared to fight. In February 211, however, Severus died and his son Caracalla took over the empire. Caracalla, eager to leave Britain and establish a power base nearer the heartlands of the empire, made peace with the locals and the Romans pulled back once more to Hadrian's Wall.

For much of the third century, things were fairly stable in Britain, although there were threats from outside, notably from the Saxons and Franks who attacked the coasts. It was probably as a result of these threats that the Romans began to strengthen their fortifications along Britain's south and east coasts. Beyond the coasts of Britain, however, the empire seemed in less good shape. Emperors fell and were replaced with great speed and there was little continuity in government.

In 284 another new emperor, Diocletian, came to the throne. Diocletian took the empire in a fresh direction by dividing it in two and appointing Maximian as co-emperor; Diocletian ruled the eastern empire, while Maximian controlled the west. Maximian saw that the threat of Saxon invasion remained and put his commander Carausius in charge of the British fleet. He hoped in so doing to halt the persistent Saxon raiders, but he failed to realize that it is difficult for a fleet to pounce on opponents when no one can predict precisely when or where the enemy is next likely to appear.

The outcome was that Carausius took to intercepting Saxon raiders on their way home from Britain. This would have proved some help, but for the fact that Carausius did not prove the loyal commander that Maximian had hoped. Instead of restoring goods taken by the raiders to their rightful owners, Carausius allegedly took some of the booty for himself. When this was discovered he avoided punishment by going on the offensive and declaring himself emperor of Britain and north-west Gaul. Carausius was allowed to get away with this usurpation for several years, but was eventually assassinated in a coup. In 296–7, a Roman naval expedition landed in Britain to clear up the trouble.

ON THE SAXON SHORE

Episodes like this show that in some ways Roman rule in Britain was rather fragile. During the fourth century, these problems continued, with further attacks from the Saxons, Picts, and Scots. These attacks impinged little on the lives of some Romanized Britons. In the country especially, villa life carried on, and many estate owners were even more prosperous than their forebears in the previous century. But there were problems in some of the towns. The forum at Wroxeter was no longer in use, London's basilica was demolished, and in other towns the public buildings were in disrepair.

By the late fourth century there was a string of coastal forts stretching from Brancaster in northern Norfolk to Portchester and Claustenum (Bitterne) in Hampshire, near the Isle of Wight. Several east-coast ports were given over to naval use, and numerous coastal forts were erected. The first of these, which had been put into service by around 230, were Brancaster and Reculver in Kent. By 370 there were further forts at Burgh Castle in Norfolk, Walton Castle in Suffolk, Bradwell in Essex, Dover and Lympne in Kent (which had been bases of the British fleet), Pevensey in Sussex, and Portchester and Bitterne in Hampshire. In addition, the Romans' first ever base in Britain, at Richborough, was also converted into a fort.

This network of fortifications became known as the Forts of the Saxon Shore. They were laid out differently from the earlier Roman forts, with massive stone walls (which could be up to ten metres tall) and projecting bastions to give a good view of the enemy and a variety of lines of fire. With their narrow gates and thick walls, these forts meant business. They were designed to show raiding Saxons that the Roman empire could still put up a formidable resistance. They also acted as strong bases for the men who manned the fleets that were meant to fight off Saxon pirates, as did two similar forts on the

European side of the Channel, at Boulogne and Oldenburg. While such structures could hardly stop Saxon piracy, they were a very solid warning to potential invaders.

PEVENSEY, EAST SUSSEX

Although it is no longer by the sea, Pevensey was a Saxon Shore fort, and one of the last to be built. It was constructed during the fourth century. Scholars once thought that the find of two tiles stamped with the name of the emperor Honorius (395–423) proved that the fort was rebuilt during his reign. These tiles were later found to be forgeries (probably planted by the renowned archaeological hoaxer Charles Dawson), but a coin of 335 found under some of the masonry shows that the fort was re-built after that date. Even after the Romans left, the locals still used the fort, unsucessfully defending it in AD 491. A massacre of the defenders followed, and Pevensey was then abandoned until the Normans arrived

and incorporated the walls into a castle.

Pevensey is also the largest of the Forts of the Saxon Shore. It covers an oval-shaped area of about 9 acres within walls that are some 3 metres thick and still rise in places to their original height of 7.5 metres. This sheer size makes Pevensey impressive. Its eleven U-shaped bastions (there were originally more) and its great gates add to this impression.

The great walls are set on foundations of flint and chalk. Above the foundations, they are built of sandstone rubble, with neat courses of ironstone and sandstone every few feet to bind the rubble courses together. Several gangs of workers were employed on the building, and the joins between the sections completed by different gangs can still be seen as changes in the sizes or shapes of the stones.

Although the walls at Pevensey are impressive, no evidence of Roman stone buildings remains inside the fort. Digs have revealed only traces of wooden buildings.

▼ THE OUTER WALLS OF PEVENSEY CASTLE, WITH THEIR COURSES OF BRICK AND STONE, WERE FAR BIGGER THAN THOSE OF EARLIER ROMAN FORTS.

▲ Some people enjoyed prosperity during the fourth century, confirmed by finds such as the Mildenhall Treasure. This dish is just one item from this collection of metalwork, dating from around AD 360.

The forts were under the command of an official who bore the title Count of the Saxon Shore. Attacks came to a head in 367, when the Count, Nectaridus, was killed and Fullofaudes, the commander of the Roman forces in Britain, was captured. The emperor had to send a succession of expeditions to restore order.

The attacks continued through to the end of the fourth century when, in 395, Honorius became emperor. At this point the empire was undergoing another major change. Continuous threats from the edges of the empire meant that the army, vital to the defence of the state, had become more and more important. The general and the imperial ministers, most of whom came from the army anyway, were often more powerful than the emperor himself. The strongest of all these military men was Flavius Stilicho, the general who virtually ruled the western empire after 395. Stilicho was by birth a Vandal, a member of one of the very tribes that had been giving Rome so much trouble. His power is an indication of how much the empire was relying on support from the non-Roman peoples of Europe by this time.

Stilicho found it hard to keep the empire under control. He sent several expeditions to Britain in the final years of the fourth century, but there were also troubles on the continent. By 402 the troops that had been sent to Britain were being moved out again to defend the heart of the empire in Europe. After this point, Rome had little involvement in Britain and, in 410, the emperor Honorius announced that henceforward the Britons would have to defend themselves. The Roman occupation of Britain was officially at an end.

It is important to understand that these threats, which contributed to the eventual break-up of the western empire, were not simply a matter of waves of 'barbarian' invaders attacking the empire from the outside. Many of those who attacked the empire were actually its own subject peoples, whose armies the Romans depended upon to keep the peace. And they were hardly 'barbarians' in any real sense of the word – many of them had been Romanized, just like the Britons.

The weakness of the empire, therefore, came as much from within as from without, and matters could be made worse for the Romans by any movement that encouraged dissent from the ruling line. All sorts of groups, rich and poor, generals and monks, might have their own interests that were not in line with those of Rome. And the problem was made worse because the empire's huge size also made it increasingly hard to control.

PORTCHESTER, HAMPSHIRE

Portchester is a Saxon Shore fort that is very unlike its neighbour, Pevensey, although it is nearly as large. Whereas Pevensey is planned in an irregular oval shape, Portchester is rectangular. The walls, which were largely refaced in the Middle Ages, are about 3 metres thick and now stand some 5.5 metres high. In some places there is no medieval refacing, and the Roman flint masonry, with its striped bonding courses of stone or tile, can still be seen. The walls are punctuated with bastions, of which fourteen out of the original twenty survive. The fort has two main gates (one of which is a medieval rebuilding) and two small gates, or posterns, now blocked.

This fort was used during the third century, but was abandoned in 296, after the usurpation and assassination of Carausius. In about 340 – around the time that the fort at Pevensey was built – a Roman garrison was once more stationed at Portchester, and this force stayed for about thirty years. Portchester then declined in importance, presumably at the expense of the fort at Bitterne, which was given stone walls in about 370. Portchester was reused by the Normans, who built a castle, with a large square keep, in one corner.

▼ THE FORT AT PORTCHESTER IS RECTANGULAR AND STILL HAS ITS MASSIVE STONE WALLS.

MASS ENTERTAINMENT

One way to distract the people from their dissension, as the Romans well knew, was to keep them well fed and entertained. The great Roman satirical poet, Juvenal, coined the most famous phrase to sum up this policy. All the people care about, he said, is 'panem et circenses', which we usually translate as 'bread and circuses', although a more accurate translation is 'bread and chariot-races'. In Rome itself people gathered at the great Circus Maximus to watch chariot-races or attended the Colosseum, the city's enormous amphitheatre, to see gory entertainments known as 'the games'.

In Britain archaeologists have found no evidence for the long racetracks called circuses which the Romans built in Europe, but the Romans were keen on horsemanship and it is likely that

▼ A RECONSTRUCTED GLADIATORIAL COMBAT.

horse and chariot-races were held in some form. Rich Romans liked to fund chariot-races. Paying for entertainments gave them kudos, but it could cost them dear. As the poet Juvenal put it, 'The praetor sits there in state, but those horses almost cost him the shirt off his back.' Another Roman poet, Martial, bemoaned the fact that the charioteers were famous, and even their horses' names were household words; poets, on the other hand, never got this sort of fame. A beautiful pottery beaker found at Colchester, decorated with images of four-horse chariots in a race, illustrates the interest shown in the sport. Many of the Roman soldiers had seen such races on the continent and would have wanted to bring them across the Channel, though not perhaps on the scale of Rome's Circus Maximus, which held a quarter of a million people.

What is certain, however, is that the Romans built amphitheatres in Britain. The remains of these structures can still be seen in many places. The military base at Caerleon, in South Wales, had an amphitheatre (see pages 36-7), as did other military centres such as Richborough, Chester, and even one auxiliary fort, Tomen-y-Mur in north-west Wales. Many towns, such as Caerwent, Cirencester, Chichester, Dorchester, and Silchester, also had amphitheatres.

▲ THIS GLADIATOR'S HELMET WAS FOUND AT HAWKEDON, SUFFOLK.

Arenas such as these must have staged a variety of entertainments. Military amphitheatres were probably used as much for drill as for games, but the bloody spectacles famous in Rome no doubt took place in Britain too. They were gruesome affairs. First, there was animal baiting. Next, hundreds of creatures were slaughtered in a grotesque parody of the hunt. Then came the gladiatorial combats. Men fought men, on foot and on horseback, to the death. Gladiators were pitched against wild beasts, from lions to elephants, until the men were gored to pieces. After each bout of fighting, slaves sprinkled fresh sand over the bloodied ground, ready for the next session to begin.

The games in Britain may well have been on a smaller scale than those in Rome itself. Animal-baiting may have played a larger part than conflicts involving expensively armed and equipped gladiators, but the find of a gladiator's helmet at Hawkedon, together with mosaics of Cupids training as gladiators at Bignor, show at least an interest in this form of entertainment. Gladiatorial combats probably took place in Britain from time to time.

THE ARENA

Roman amphitheatres were usually oval in plan. In the centre was the arena (the word arena comes from the Latin *harena*, sand, after the sand with which the ground was covered). The rest of the structure was taken up with tiers of seats, raised higher towards the back to give everyone a good view of the spectacle. By the standards of the huge continental amphitheatres, such as those in Rome and Verona, British amphitheatres were quite small. Instead of the impressive stone-built structures of Italy, with their rows of arches and labyrinths of underground cells and passages, Romano-British amphitheatres were based on earth banks with wooden seats. One of the largest amphitheatres in Britain, at Dorchester, was 103 metres across and contained an arena measuring about 58 by 52 metres, which made it large enough for the several thousand spectators that it had to accommodate.

Many British amphitheatres seem to have been built during the decades after the conquest. The one at Caerleon was put up in around AD 90; Silchester's amphitheatre was built at some time between AD 50 and 75. The Colosseum in Rome was being built at this time, so in parts of Britain, as in the empire's capital, amphitheatres and games must have been an important part of life.

At Silchester, the amphitheatre may have been built at the behest of Togidubnus, the highly Romanized local king who probably lived in the palace at Fishbourne, but the structure certainly outlasted him. Archaeologists have discovered that it was repaired during the second century, that it was enlarged in the third century, when a new arena wall was built, and that it was probably used for much of the fourth century.

The Romans staged these entertainments, then, throughout their occupation of Britain. Local leaders could achieve support by sponsoring events in the arena, and the Roman rulers no doubt valued the whole exercise as a way of keeping a potentially rebellious people happy. A boisterous crowd in the amphitheatre was better than a riotous mob fighting on the streets or storming a legionary base.

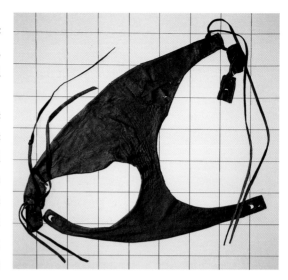

▲ THESE LEATHER BIKINI BOTTOMS WERE FOUND IN LONDON AND MAY HAVE BELONGED TO A YOUNG ACROBAT.

THE INVENTIONS OF HERO

Not all Roman entertainments were as gruesome as the games. Roman engineers and scientists also produced a number of ingenious mechanical devices to amuse and delight. Many of these were invented or perfected by a famous scientist who came from the opposite end of the empire to Britain. His name was Hero, and he lived in Alexandria, in Egypt. Like many Alexandrians, Hero was of Greek extraction. So he cannot be called a Roman inventor. Yet without the vast Roman empire, which stretched from Northern Africa to Southern Scotland, Hero's ideas would have had little chance of reaching Northern Europe. The spread of his ideas is a good example of how the Roman communication network disseminated innovations around the world. Hero's inventions were many and diverse. They ranged from an early form of steam engine to a mechanical puppet theatre. Two of them, a form of organ and early slot machine, travelled widely and may have been known in Britain.

MECHANICAL MUSIC

There is evidence that the Romans used their technological skills to make their entertainment in the arena even more exciting. Some of the first mechanical musical instruments were perfected in the Roman empire. The emperor Nero's favourite musical instrument was the water organ or *hydraulis*, the world's first keyboard instrument and early ancestor of the church organ.

The water organ seems to have been reasonably common in the Roman empire and had appeared by the late first century BC, when Vitruvius wrote a description of the device. It worked using compressed air to blow a series of pipes, just like a modern organ. It was known as the water organ because water was used in the air reservoir. This reservoir consisted of a cauldron of air up-ended in a vessel of water. Air pressure on the exposed surface of the water kept the air in the cauldron at constant pressure, so that when the air entered the pipes it always did so at a uniform rate. The organist had an assistant who worked a bellows or a pump to keep the cauldron supplied with pressurized air.

Vitruvius included a long passage in his *Ten Books on Architecture* detailing how the water organ worked. He describes the air reservoir, the pipes, and the mechanism that allows the player to control the amount of air entering the pipes, and the way this is linked to a keyboard. It is a complex mechanism of stop-cocks, levers, and linkages, and it gives Vitruvius some trouble. Finally, he admits, 'With my best efforts I have striven to set forth an obscure subject clearly in writing, but the theory of it is not easy, nor readily understood by all, save only those who have had some practice in things of this kind.'

The water organ was popular, producing, as Vitruvius says, 'resonant sounds in a great variety of melodies conforming to the laws of music'. It was apparently used at celebrations such as weddings and banquets, and in state ceremonies, as well as at the games. Not surprisingly, given his interest in mechanical devices, Hero of Alexandria was also fascinated by the water organ. He developed a version which did away with the need for an organist's assistant. In Hero's design, the air pump that supplied

◀ A RELIEF SHOWS THE TYPE OF MASK WORN BY ACTORS IN THE ROMAN THEATRE.

◀ A MOSAIC DEPICTS THE WATER ORGAN – THE WORLD'S FIRST KEYBOARD INSTRUMENT AND EARLY ANCESTOR OF THE CHURCH ORGAN.

the pipes was powered by a windmill! There is no evidence that this version of the instrument caught on, but hand-pumped water organs seem often to have been used during gladiatorial contests and other games in the arena, as well as to accompany performances in the theatre.

Coins in the slot

The slot machine was one of Hero's most surprising inventions. The idea was simple and very modern. You put a small coin into a slot and the machine would dispense something, in this case some holy water that was required for ritual washing before making an offering at a temple.

The device worked by means of a carefully balanced lever. The user dropped a coin through a small slot on the front of the machine. The coin fell on to a small pan on the end of a beam that was delicately balanced, like a see-saw. As the coin dropped in, the pan moved downwards and the other end of the beam shot up. As this end was raised it pulled a wire, opening a valve and letting some water out of the machine. At the same time, the coin slid off the moving pan, so that the balance reset itself to its original position, and the valve closed once more, cutting off the stream of water. While all this was happening, the machine had dispensed enough water to wash the user's hands, and at the end of the day the priests could empty the machine and add the money to the temple's coffers.

TECHNOLOGY TO THE RESCUE?

At least one Roman writer, the anonymous author of a fourth-century book called *De Rebus Bellicus* ('Concerning Military Matters'), thought that technology might be used in a much more serious way. He suggests that new inventions might come to the rescue of the Roman empire when it came to quelling barbarian invasions. At the beginning of the book the writer describes the threat from these people, saying: 'Barbarians are assailing every frontier.' But the writer understands that there are also problems within the empire. In particular, the army is not strong enough and recruitment is difficult, especially as there are a range of classes and professions, from bureaucrats to slaves, who are exempt from military service. The writer diagnoses other difficulties with the army too. He says that it is much too expensive to run and puts a crippling burden on the Roman tax system. The writer therefore suggests a series of solutions that use technology to save on manpower. His recommendations, which largely seem to have gone unheeded, range from improved siege engines to a number of extraordinary new engines of war.

One of the most remarkable of these is a boat powered by oxen. The boat described had several pairs of paddle wheels, rather like those on a Mississippi steamer, and required two oxen to drive each pair. The beasts were harnessed at either end of a pole. As they walked around in circles, the pole turned a huge gear, which in a crown-and-pinion arrangement turned a second gear on an axle that bore two paddle wheels. These wheels were designed rather like the undershot water wheels described by Vitruvius. The writer does not say how many oxen there were, but mentions more than one pair. The ship needed to accommodate the oxen and the gears needed to power the wheels would have been large, so it is doubtful whether the craft would have been very efficient. The vessel was probably never built, but it is a testimony to the Roman faith in technology that someone thought of suggesting this solution to the empire's failing grip on the high seas.

Another problem with the army was that they carried with them everything they needed, from basic rations to the parts

needed to build a bridge over any river they came to. The author of *De Rebus Bellicus* suggests a different approach to crossing a river – an inflatable bridge. Made with animal skins, it could be carried by two or three people and 50 mules. Such an idea sounds extraordinarily modern, but it could have worked – after all, the ancient Assyrians had used inflated animal skins to make rafts – but, like the other ideas in *De Rebus Bellicus*, it seems to have been ignored.

ROMAN CONCRETE

The Romans seemed to prefer to rely on tried and tested solutions to their problems.

There was one building material, for example, that the Romans introduced which they used extensively – concrete. Concrete was especially useful when the empire was threatened with attack because it made it easy to build strong fortifications at speed.

Like so many of the innovations that the invaders brought with them, concrete was not strictly a Roman invention. The first mortared walls seem to have been built in Campania, the area in southern Italy settled by Greeks and Etruscans, during the fourth and third centuries BC. In the third century BC, the concept of mortar and concrete was spreading to the Roman world, and to Rome itself.

To begin with, the masons of Pompeii built walls made up of outer skins of limestone blocks with an inner filling of rubble. The bits of rubble were at first held together with a binding clay, but the Pompeiians discovered that by mixing lime with a volcanic ash called pozzolana they could make a mixture that set hard and strong: one of the most effective forms of cement ever produced.

▲ THE SUCESSFUL TEST OF THE PRINCIPLE OF THE INFLATABLE BRIDGE. THE IDEA WAS TO USE INFLATABLE ANIMAL SKINS.

▶ THE RUBBLE CORES OF THE WALLS AT RICHBOROUGH ARE STILL HELD TOGETHER BY ROMAN CONCRETE.

This pozzolana, a reddish-coloured material named after Pozzuoli, near the Bay of Naples where it was found, was a key ingredient because it allowed the mixture to set rock-hard even when soaked in water. Roman builders were the first to realize its huge potential.

Ancient writers wondered at this magic substance. Pliny, in his *Natural History*, was typically impressed: 'For who could not marvel enough that on the hills of Puteoli [sic] there exists a dust…that, as soon as it comes into contact with the waves of the sea and is submerged, becomes a single stone mass, impregnable to the waves and every day stronger…' Vitruvius, too, sang the praises of pozzolana, devoting an entire chapter of his *Ten Books on Architecture* to the substance and noting the 'astonishing results' it makes possible. By adding broken rocks to the pozzolana cement, they produced concrete, a building material that was strong, versatile, and easy to make.

Concrete had huge potential and the Romans used it in many ways. Firstly and most simply, it enabled them to produce massive walls at speed, without highly skilled labour, by mixing concrete and rubble. Such masonry could form the filling of a thick wall that was finished with neat stone blocks or brickwork. So strong was such a concrete core that on many Roman sites it still remains, long after the outer stones or bricks have been removed and recycled. For building quickly, for example to create massive-walled fortifications, concrete was ideal.

The new building material was very useful in any construction project where it was necessary to create curves. As we have seen, the Romans liked to build rooms with apsidal, or semicircular, ends and alcoves. Concrete, with its plastic quality, was ideal for creating these shapes.

Concrete was also perfect for vaulting, another area of construction where curves were of the essence. Making a vault with solid stones was a difficult and time-consuming process, which needed workers skilled in both masonry and carpentry. Massive supporting timbers, called centring, had to be put up before the masonry could be laid. Concrete cut down on the amount of timber required, together with the time needed. In one method, the carpenter was the first to start work. But instead of building a large supporting structure consisting of a heavy wooden frame covered with thick planking, he put up a much more lightweight frame.

The new Roman concrete had one other supreme advantage. Because it set hard under water, absorbing moisture like a sponge, it was invaluable in bridge-building. Before the use of concrete, stone bridges were difficult to build. Either they had to be very small, like prehistoric British 'clapper' bridges that had uprights made of large single stones, or they relied on elaborate masonry techniques to fit blocks so precisely together that they did not need mortar. More often than not, builders had to be content with a wooden bridge, which of course had a limited life-span. With concrete, proper, large-scale masonry bridges were at last viable. Fragments of one or two stone bridges have been found by archaeologists in Britain. At Piercebridge, Durham, for example, the stones of some of the bridge piers can still be seen, and there are quite substantial remains of a stone bridge abutment at Chesters, on Hadrian's Wall. But to see complete examples of Roman bridge-building one has to go to Europe, where structures such as the Bridge of Augustus at Rimini, Italy, or the bridge over the Tagus at Alcantara, Spain, show what Roman bridge-builders could achieve. However, there is plenty of evidence in Britain for the Roman skill in concrete-making, in the walls of forts, villas, and other buildings at archaeological sites all over the country.

AFTER THE ROMANS

When the Romans withdrew, the effects of their rule of Britain did not disappear immediately. They left behind them a population of Romanized Britons, most of whom no doubt wanted to retain the wealth and comfort they had enjoyed under their European rulers. Life in some towns carried on, if not exactly as it had before then at least in a similar way. Archaeologists have found that urban life, especially in well-fortified towns that could stand up to incursions from invading Angles and Saxons, continued well into the fifth century. Verulamium, Cirencester, and Silchester have revealed this pattern. Verulamium, for example, was visited in 429 by St Germanus, a bishop from Auxerre who came to campaign against heresy. Germanus found the town well governed, with a rich upper class. In the country, too, the good life continued for many Romanized Britons, with post-Roman occupation in evidence at many villa sites.

But Britain was eventually taken over by new rulers – invading Jutes, Angles, and Saxons who saw little advantage in preserving the Romanized lifestyle of the place they were taking over. So in the centuries after the Romans left, much of their legacy disappeared too. Towns declined and villas were abandoned. Skills such as mosaic-making were lost. Timber became the main material for building once more. Knowledge of the Romans' elaborate signalling techniques and surveying methods disappeared. Above all, the Romans' talent for large-scale organization was forgotten as the island divided into separate kingdoms.

Writers used to speak of this post-Roman period as the 'Dark Ages', when Roman civilization was forgotten in a cultural night that lasted for centuries, but historians now emphasize that the Saxons had an impressive culture of their own. Some aspects of this culture, indeed, were influenced by the Romans: the Church preserved the Latin language, for example, and when the Saxons built in stone, they used arches and vaults influenced by the architecture of Rome. Other Roman innovations, most notably the road network, remained in place for all to use. But much Roman technology did disappear in post-Roman times. Lighthouses and prefabricated buildings, odometers and slot machines, reaping machines and military machines, arenas and theatres – all these were lost with the Romans, only to be reinvented hundreds of years later, or to be rediscovered by modern archaeologists searching for evidence of the rich Roman civilization.

BIBLIOGRAPHY

This bibliography lists the works that have been most useful in the preparation of this book. The dates given are those of the edition used. Most of the books listed have their own bibliographies, enabling the interested reader to pursue the subject further. In addition, the academic journal *Britannia*, published annually by the Society for the Promotion of Roman Studies, covers the most recent developments in the archaeology of Roman Britain.

GENERAL

Jean-Pierre Adam, *Roman Building: Materials and Techniques* (Routledge, 1999)

Joan Alcock, *Life in Roman Britain* (Batsford, 1996)

F R Cowell, *Everyday Life in Ancient Rome* (Batsford, 1973)

M Daumas, *A History of Technology and Invention* (John Murray, 1969)

Stephen Hill and Stanley Ireland, *Roman Britain* (Bristol Classical Press, 1996)

Henry Hodges, *Technology in the Ancient World* (Penguin, 1971)

John W Humphrey, John P Oleson, and Andrew N Sherwood, *Greek and Roman Technology: A Sourcebook* (Routledge, 1998)

G D B Jones and D J Mattingly, *An Atlas of Roman Britain* (Blackwell, 1990)

David E Johnston (ed), *Discovering Roman Britain* (Shire, 1993)

J G Landels, *Engineering in the Ancient World* (Constable, 1997)

Ordnance Survey, *Map of Roman Britain*

T W Potter, *Roman Britain* (British Museum Press, 1997)

I A Richmond and Malcolm Todd, *Roman Britain* (Penguin, 1995)

Peter Salway, *The Oxford Illustrated History of Roman Britain* (Oxford University Press, 1993)

Frank Sear, *Roman Architecture* (Routledge, 1982)

Plantagenet Somerset Fry, *Roman Britain* (David and Charles, 1984)

K D White, *Greek and Roman Technology* (Thames and Hudson, 1984)

Roger J A Wilson, *A Guide to the Roman Remains in Britain* (Constable, 1988) Shire,

INVASION

Paul Bidwell, *Roman Forts in Britain* (B T Batsford/ English Heritage, 1997)

John Peddie, *The Roman War Machine* (Alan Sutton, 1994)

C M Gilliver, *The Roman Art of War* (Tempus, 1999)

G Webster, *The Roman Army* (Black, 1985)

ARTERIES OF THE EMPIRE

Richard W Bagshawe, *Roman Roads* (Shire, 1979)

Raymond Chevallier, *Roman Roads* (Batsford, 1976)

D E Johnston, *An Illustrated History of Roman Roads in Britain* (Spurbooks, 1979)

I D Margary, *Roman Roads in Britain* (John Baker, 1973)

EDGE OF EMPIRE

A K Bowman, *Life and Letters on the Roman Frontier* (British Museum Press, 1994)

D J Breeze, *The Northern Frontiers of Rome* (Batsford, 1982)

Guy de la Bédoyére, *Hadrian's Wall: History & Guide* (Tempus, 1998)

James Forde-Johnston, *Hadrian's Wall* (BCA, 1977)

S Johnson, *Hadrian's Wall* (Batsford, 1989)

BUILDING BRITAIN

B C Burnham and John Wacher, *The 'Small Towns' of Roman Britain* (Batsford, 1990)

A L F Rivet, *Town and Country in Roman Britain* (Hutchinson, 1964)

John Wacher, *The Towns of Roman Britain* (Routledge, 1995)

LIFE OF LUXURY

Barry Cunliffe, *Fishbourne Roman Palace* (Tempus, 1998)

Peter Johnson, *Romano-British Mosaics* (Shire, 1982)

David E Johnston, *Roman Villas* (Shire, 1994)

Roger Ling, *Romano-British Wall Painting* (Shire, 1985)

John Percival, *The Roman Villa* (B T Batsford, 1988)

A L F Rivet, *The Roman Villa in Britain* (Routledge and Kegan Paul, 1969)

Tony Rook, *Roman Baths in England* (Shire, 1992)

AHEAD OF THEIR TIME

A S Esmonde-Cleary, *The Ending of Roman Britain* (Batsford, 1989)

Michael Grant, *The Fall of the Roman Empire* (Weidenfeld, 1990)

WEBSITES

www.ancientsites.com/~Lucius_Aelius/
www.britainexpress.com/History/
www.english-heritage.org.uk

www.hadrians-wall.org.uk
www.thebritishmuseum.ac.uk
www.24hourmuseum.org.uk

INDEX